THE PARTY BIBLE

I dedicate this book to my long-suffering daughter,
Tallulah Rendall, all the special women in my life,
and my party male-mates.

First published in book form in Great Britain 2003
by Artnik
26 Pont Street
London SW1X 0AB

ISBN 1 903906 19 9

Acknowledgements
The author wishes to thank the many friends whose encouragement and contributions have
helped to make this book possible, most especially Dame Shirley Bassey and Ivana Trump, and
gratefully acknowledges all those who have allowed their photographs or illustrations to be used.

Every reasonable attempt has been made to contact all photographers;
we thank them for their contribution.
The extract from *Party Cocktails* by Ian Wisniewski is reproduced by kind permission of the
publisher, Conran Octopus.

Cartoons and line-drawings by Liz Brewer (except where stated otherwise)
Design and page make-up: Linda Wade
Editor: Elizabeth Shaw-Hardie
Indexer: Oula Jones

Printed in Bulgaria by Demax PLC

THE PARTY BIBLE

All you want to know but never dared ask!

Written and illustrated by
LIZ BREWER

Artnik
LONDON

'You have to have a dream
… and you have to make that
dream happen'

Liz Brewer
The Fame Game 1994

Michael and Sophie Hanna's *Bad Taste*
party invitation.
Illustration: Peter Solkel

'A social gathering of invited guests typically involving drinking, eating and entertainment'

Oxford English Dictionary:

definition of a 'party'

introduction

When contemplating having a party the questions uppermost in most people's minds are:

- How? – How best to suit wallets and match fantasies?
- Where? – Should the occasion be held at home, in an unusual location, or shared with others?
- With whom? – Will it be a quiet family affair, a street party, a ball, or a fabulous fantasia?
- Should we hire, borrow or buy?

It has been my pleasure over the past twenty years to answer these kinds of question for many friends and clients, fulfilling their wishes and dreams, while bearing in mind budgets. Occasionally, when strapped for cash, I have given simple parties such as picnics in the park, but I have also organised the most lavish extravaganzas imaginable.

I adore parties, and I love to create and organise them. I particularly enjoy the freedom they give to dress up, be with friends, and live out dreams with style and panache. In my opinion the world of 'party' begins when people arrive home, take off their working expressions, and change from their daily uniform into something that reflects their personality or fantasy. It is my belief that parties are the space where we like to be our true selves, to relax, exchange tittle-tattle or indulge in deep philosophical debate. It is a different world, divorced from the mundane reality of daily life, where we can enjoy a feeling of freedom and take pleasure in satisfying our senses. Planning a party is about creating that other world. It takes artistry and inventiveness; it takes the willingness to be dashing and, on occasion, daring.

I have arranged parties in many different locations, from gatherings on the sandbanks of the Zambezi and pirate parties on yachts in the south of France to sensational soirées in the stately homes of England. Even now I am in the early planning stages for the first party in space. (This is for Buzz Aldrin, who with Neil Armstrong was the first astronaut to set foot on the moon.) Along the way I have learned that celebrating is not necessarily a rich man's frivolity, and the amount of money spent is not the yardstick by which to measure the success of a party. An inventive host with a limited budget can create parties that have more magic than the extravaganzas of the nouveau riche. The secret of throwing perfect parties is the care and attention that you put into every detail to honour and delight your guests.

I acquired my party-giving experience the hard way, learning through my mistakes. Usually everything goes according to plan, but not always. Occasionally I have hit 'walls' – those seemingly insurmountable problems when you have to find a way to turn a minus into a plus – and I have learned that the secret is to retain a sense of humour even when things are at their worst. There is always a way out of even the deepest hole – often it is to stop digging and start laughing.

In this book, I have pulled together the knowledge and wisdom I have gained from years of creating parties, including the nuts and bolts of organisation and the secrets of how to make a party a memorable occasion. Here are my dos and don'ts of successful organisation, my shortcuts for creating the maximum effect for the minimum outlay of cash, and my tips for negotiating every area of this complex and sometimes frightening world of entertaining. Turn these pages and begin to discover how to transform even the simplest idea into exciting results.

inspiration

'Let's give a party!' somebody says, and everyone replies, 'What a great idea! Let's have a party!' Suddenly there is a delicious tingle in the air, a feeling of expectancy that something exciting is happening.

In between this first great burst of inspiration and the moment when the last guest leaves, there is an ocean of uncharted waters. They may appear calm and easy to navigate, but they can be filled with unforeseen perils that need a steady hand on the tiller.

How does one start? When asked this question, I always advise: 'Begin in your mind, dream your perfect party, and let your imagination run wild.' If you get stuck and no brilliant ideas come flooding in, scour the magazines, look at parties others have given, and pick up whatever inspiration or tips you can. Whether or not you have a great deal of money to spend, anything is possible with imagination and planning.

At this embryonic stage, your idea is like a tiny seed, which you must nurture and cherish – it's a long way from having complete form. There are so many things to consider, it's enough to give anyone a panic attack! To help you avoid this, I have created the Party Tree (*see* pages 12–13). Each of its branches represents a different and significant aspect of a party and is laden with an assortment of ideas for bringing people together to enjoy a great event.

The important thing is to dream …

CELESTIAL SUN

GUESTS' DUTIES

APPENDIX I

DRESS CODES

KNOWING WHEN TO LEAVE

PRESENTS

THANK YOUS

GOODBYES

COOK OR CHEF

GREETERS

8. STAFF & HELPERS

CLEANERS

ATTENDANTS

TOASTMASTERS

DOORMEN

TOASTS

DRINKS

EQUIPMENT

CAKES

MENUS

6. CATERING

SUPPLIERS

ADULT TOYS

BALLOONS

FLOWERS

4. DECOR & THEME

FANCY DRESS

LIGHTING

THEMES

MAILING INVITATIONS

WHO TO INVITE

2. THE GUESTS

TRAVEL

INVITATION FORMATS

DRESS

GUEST LISTS

INSP

PARTY

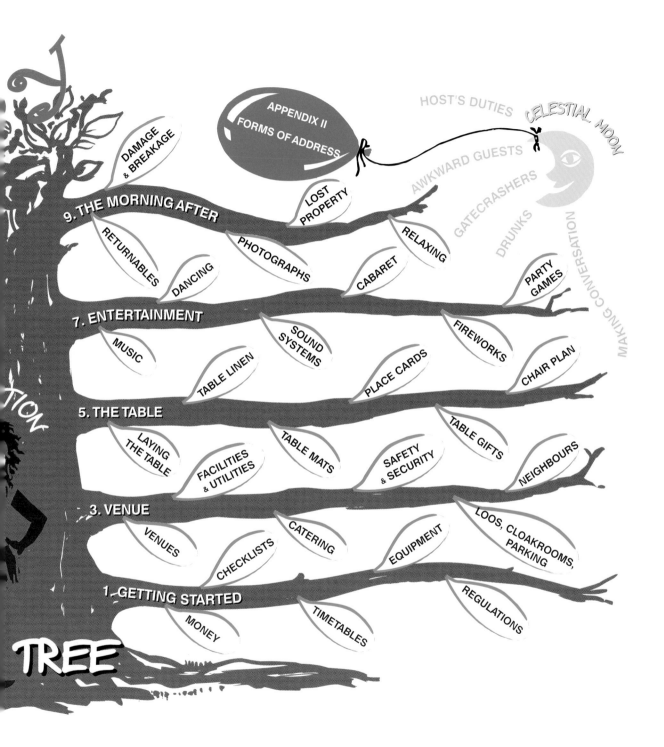

TREE

1. GETTING STARTED
- MONEY
- TIMETABLES
- REGULATIONS

3. VENUE
- VENUES
- CHECKLISTS
- CATERING
- EQUIPMENT
- LOOS, CLOAKROOMS, PARKING

5. THE TABLE
- LAYING THE TABLE
- FACILITIES & UTILITIES
- TABLE MATS
- SAFETY & SECURITY
- TABLE GIFTS
- NEIGHBOURS

7. ENTERTAINMENT
- MUSIC
- TABLE LINEN
- SOUND SYSTEMS
- PLACE CARDS
- FIREWORKS
- CHAIR PLAN

9. THE MORNING AFTER
- RETURNABLES
- DANCING
- PHOTOGRAPHS
- CABARET
- RELAXING
- PARTY GAMES

- DAMAGE & BREAKAGE
- LOST PROPERTY

APPENDIX II
FORMS OF ADDRESS

HOST'S DUTIES
AWKWARD GUESTS
GATECRASHERS
DRUNKS
MAKING CONVERSATION
CELESTIAL MOON

'*Whatever you can do or dream you can, begin it… boldness has genius, power and magic in it*'

Goethe

getting started – the nitty-gritty

MONEY MATTERS

Budget

Before doing anything else, draw up an approximate budget covering all the obvious outgoings. Sifting through the pages of this book, studying the Party Tree (*see* pages 12–13) and checking through the list of equipment below, will help you to ensure that you take into account all the necessary items. Also make provision for possible hidden extras, and be aware that when you receive a quote it does not always include VAT.

If you find that the anticipated costs are exceeding your planned budget, you will need to do one or all of the following:

- Revise the budget (if that is possible).
- Compromise on some of the details.
- Be prepared to improvise (in some of the ways described in this book) so that you can avoid some of the costs.

Bear in mind that buying in bulk is more economical (non-perishable items can always be reserved for future events if you do not use everything this time); and it is also worth talking to your various suppliers to negotiate discounts wherever possible, especially for large orders.

Having decided your budget, you may find it an advantage – especially if you are planning a large event – to open a separate account at your bank to use solely for party expenditure. This will give you a more accurate picture of how the finances are going as you go along.

Terms and Payments

Credit and payment terms will vary from one supplier to another. However, the following serves as a general guide:

■ Quotations from suppliers that are confirmed and accepted in writing by the client are normally valid for three months from the date of quotation.
■ A deposit is normal, although the necessity for this will depend on the relationship between the supplier and the client.
■ Settlement of accounts must generally be made between fourteen days and one month.

It is important to read any small print carefully, paying particular attention to any cancellation clauses, limitations of liability or *force majeure* (believe me the unexpected often happens – floods and bomb scares, for example!)

Note whether the supplier takes responsibility for the safety of any food or equipment once it is delivered to the client. Usually it is you, the client, who takes responsibility for any equipment supplied, but this is not always the case. Unless you have adequate insurance, take out extra insurance to cover the possibility that the food and equipment disappear or get damaged (otherwise so too will your budget!).

If you have any complaints, voice them immediately directly to the supplier and confirm in writing not more than forty-eight hours after the event.

VAT and Tax

If your event is to do with your business or connected to a registered charity it is very likely that you may be entitled to some tax relief, and a VAT rebate may be in order. If in doubt check with an accountant.

Cash Float

You will need a cash float, especially on the day of the event. Even if your party is a private event unconnected with fundraising, staff or performers may need change for taxis and so on, or you may need cash for tips.

TIMETABLES AND CHECKLISTS

Once you have decided on a date, it is a good idea to make a detailed timetable and checklist, showing a work plan of all that is necessary to put in hand right up until the moment guests arrive. This way you will avoid overlooking any vital ingredient. It is sensible to order and organise as much as possible well in advance. Delays happen for various reasons, not least that the items you require are out of stock with the supplier. The more notice you give suppliers the better. For a large event, also make a 'one-week-before' timetable to check everything is going according to plan.

To make a useful timetable and checklist I generally advise people to dream the event. Relax, close your eyes, and go through the motions of the party. Put yourself in the shoes of a guest and visualise everything from the moment they receive the invitation, to the moments they arrive, park the car, enter the front door, visit the cloakroom, meet the host and are given their first drink, and so on and so on, until the moment they leave. As you go through this process, jot down in sequence a list of everything important. I have used this method for many years and, although I have much experience and information at my fingertips, I still go through this process with every event.

On the actual day have a detailed checklist and go through it meticulously.

Christopher Biggins from the *Prize Guys Celebrity Auction* catalogue.

Photograph: Adrian Houston

ATTENTION TO DETAIL

A wise old man once told me that attention to detail is one of the secrets of success. I believe that
is true – I have been trying to prove it ever since!

It is amazing how many little items are overlooked or forgotten. So keep a notepad and pencil on you at all times and, whenever you think of something important, write it down. You may well find that, like me, you end up writing lists of lists, but at least you will not keep worrying about what you might be forgetting.

EQUIPMENT

Deciding what equipment you will need is a very tedious part of organising parties, but it is vitally important and therefore must be taken seriously if no essential detail is to be overlooked.

The caterers usually provide banqueting equipment. If a marquee is being used, they can also provide the tables, chairs and portable flooring. But if you decide to do your own catering then, with large numbers especially, hiring equipment makes sense. Some catering companies will advise and supply your needs even if they are not providing the food and drink. Nowadays, many restaurants also hire out crockery and other utensils; the leaders have some stylish selections superior to the normal canteen-type ware. Of course, if you are organising a 'Bad Taste' party such as my good friends Sophie and Michael Hanna did for Sophie's fiftieth birthday, you will not be seeking stylish accoutrements.

Checklist of Equipment

If you decide to do your own catering, you will probably have to hire many of the necessary pieces of equipment. You will need some or all of the following items:

General
    Air conditioning units
    Industrial heaters
    Portable flooring (if there is no dance floor at the chosen venue)
    Cloakroom equipment and lavatory accessories

Food and drink
    Tables and chairs
    Serving tables
    Linen
    Cold storage units

Heating units/hot plates/ovens
Crockery
Cutlery
Glasses
Serving dishes
Ice buckets
Jugs
Containers
Trays
Dispense bar

Decorations and props
Balloons
Flowers
Fancy dress accessories (e.g., make-up, hats, etc.)

Lighting and entertainment
Control systems and sound systems
Adaptors if insufficient power points
Spotlights
Laser beams
Torches and flares
Fairy lights
Floodlighting
Candles, candle holders and candelabra, nightlights
Fireworks

Cleaning
Selection of cloths, kitchen towel and cleaning products
Dustpan and brush, mop, vacuum cleaner, and so on
Plastic bins and bin liners – and plenty of them (in case you need to bag any difficult people!)

RULES AND REGULATIONS

Especially when organising a gathering in a place that is not a recognised events venue, you will need to contact all the relevant authorities to check that your plans will not breach any rules and regulations. It is important to find out early in the planning stage what regulations you must comply with as these may affect your decision to use a particular venue. For example, there may be restrictions on the numbers that may attend your event and on the numbers of musicians or other artists and entertainers that are permitted to perform at your chosen venue. Restrictions and the need for special licences are especially likely if the occasion is some form of fundraiser and attended by people buying entrance tickets. The authorities will also guide you on a number of other relevant points, including:

- Licensing hours.
- Minimum facilities required for the number of guests.
- Noise levels.
- Rubbish collection.
- Fire regulations.

Even if you are hiring an established licensed venue, check the licensing hours. It is possible that the owner, you or the organiser will have to apply for an extension to the hours so that your guests will be able to drink and dance after the normal licensing hours. You should also check that the venue is licensed for the number of performing artists you want to have. Contact the Licensing Department at the Town Hall.

If you are having a large gathering somewhere other than at an established venue, contact the Health and Safety Executive of the local council who will advise you on a number of health and safety issues and tell you what facilities are required to comply with regulations. There is in fact a 'Guide to Health, Safety and Welfare at Music or Similar Events', which can be requested from the local council or accessed on line (by subscription) on: *www.hsedirect.com*. Chapter 14 of this guide refers to sanitary conveniences, and says that the minimum requirements should be agreed with the local authority found at either the Town Hall or the District Borough Council. These requirements depend on: the nature of the event; the audience profile, and the type of venue. However, having checked this guide myself, I consider that it seriously underestimates the number of lavatories required for attendees (it suggests that one loo per hundred attendees is enough!). So use common sense – no one likes queuing for the loo.

You will also need to find out about noise levels, and if you do not want to be directly responsible for the removal of rubbish to the local tip you will need to make special arrangements (through the Town Hall) for collection after the event (there may be a small charge for this) .If you are not sure which authorities deal with what, contact your local council who should be able to advise you.

You may also need to contact the police and the local fire authority to give details of the planned event. It is in any case advisable and courteous to contact the police, especially if you are expecting a large number of guests. If, despite everything, the police do turn up: be polite and, even if you're not, act sober. Most importantly, agree with everything they say (even if you go on to ignore most of it).

Petrina Khashoggi and me at the Hannas' Bad Taste party.

*A great party is the result
of a good mix!*

branch 2

the guests

If you have a good mixture of people, your party is bound to succeed. It won't matter if the marquee blows away, the champagne is flat or the cabaret flops, the right guests will make it a great event. Think about who you would like to have around. After all, most people hope to share special occasions with fun and fascinating people.

Make certain you choose the people you really want as guests, that is to say the ones who you are sure will inject vitality and make a contribution towards enhancing the atmosphere. Sociable, animated guests will help to create a party of parties – and memories that could last a lifetime. If your party is one that you want to be especially memorable, there is little point in inviting guests if they are known party poopers or make a habit of putting a damper on the atmosphere – even if you feel you ought to include them in order to return hospitality. One of your other guests could unwittingly become the focus of their attention and end up having a terrible time. So leave the uninspiring guests for another occasion.

Previous page: Liz Brewer, Henry Reid, Anton Kristensen and companion at Henry's 40th birthday party.
Photograph: Stanley Hurwitz

GUEST LISTS

Make an initial list of the guests that you would like to invite, being sure to include different categories, such as:

- Close family and good friends.
- Singles and doubles.
- 'Sugar and Spice'.
- Young and fun-loving wrinklies or even crinklies!

One of the ways to make your guest list more exciting is to inject some new blood. Invite a neighbour you have not met or someone you want to know but have never had the opportunity to meet. For a special occasion, an unexpected invitation is likely to be welcomed with an exceptional level of good will and heightened curiosity. I enjoy mixing 'sugar and spice' enormously so I frequently invite varied and unusual guests. When possible, I also have a team of loyal supporters around who will occasionally come to my rescue: characters such as my interior designer, Robin Anderson, who gives me additional ideas for the decor, and 'TV Super Chef' Brian Turner who has saved my bacon on many occasions by managing to transform and multiply two loaves and five fishes when more people than expected turned up.

Sort out those who you feel prefer to be single and encourage them to play the party flirt. Guests who enjoy dabbling in a little mild flirtation add a certain sizzle. However, be tactful: never presume a single person wants to come alone to your party. Often, unless specifically invited to bring a partner, they assume they have been asked along singly in order to balance numbers and might then give your party a miss because they feel they cannot bring a guest.

If you think your invitation list looks a little flat, put your invited guests to work. Invite them to bring a new friend who they think might be a valuable addition and add an extra zing and razzmatazz to your event. Flatter them by saying something like, 'You always seem to have such fascinating and interesting people around you – do bring one to my party.' Instantly you will have an attractive addition to your guest list.

Numbers

Often it is a good idea to check your guests' availability before sending out invitations. Guests like to be surprised, but it can be helpful to find out if they are available on the date that you have in mind, especially if you have a minimum number to make the party work and a strict maximum. It will give you an overall picture of who can or cannot attend and allow you to make adjustments to the guest list if necessary.

When deciding on the number of invitations to print, remember it is better to do too many than not enough, and as you will discover the extra cost of printing by the fifty or the hundred is minimal. Depending on the size and quality of your guest list, a ratio of one in three acceptances is the average norm. As a rule I print double the number of invitations I require, so a hundred guests equals 200 invitations. You will be amazed at how quickly they are used up. Also there may be a number of people to whom you would like to send the invitation even though you are fully aware that they will be unable to attend – it is still flattering to be asked, I always think.

Sorting the sheep from the goats!

Split your list of guests into the 'A' and 'B' list. Make a couple of copies and keep the spare list somewhere safe. You will need these if you receive the dismal news of a polite refusal. An 'A' and 'B' list means you are always prepared in the event you need to invite alternative guests. This may sound somewhat harsh but at times it is a necessity. You will in any case need these lists to help you keep track of acceptances and refusals.

Sorting the sheep from the goats.

WRITING INVITATIONS

An invitation card is the simplest and most informative way of providing your intended guests.with all the relevant details. The current trend is for invitations to be unusual or intriguing – the implication being that the more inventive or inspiring the invitation, the more interesting the party (which is not necessarily the case, of course, although original invitations do make an impression). There is nothing wrong with being imaginative so long as you cover all the facts. For this reason the basic wording of the so-called 'formal invitation' is often the easiest and simplest guide: the wording suits the purpose and it is foolproof. But there are no hard and fast rules, so don't be bullied by convention.

The facts that need to be spelt out are:

A standard formal invitation. (The name of the guest is handwritten.)

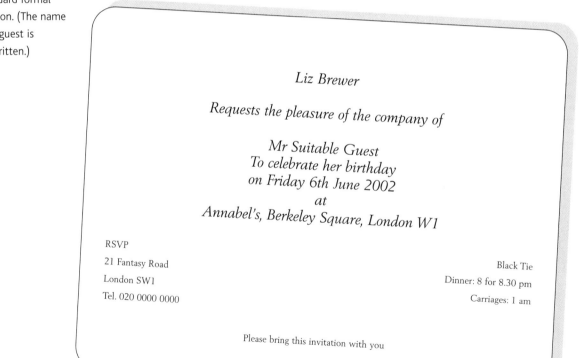

Liz Brewer

Requests the pleasure of the company of

Mr Suitable Guest
To celebrate her birthday
on Friday 6th June 2002
at
Annabel's, Berkeley Square, London W1

RSVP
21 Fantasy Road
London SW1
Tel. 020 0000 0000

Black Tie
Dinner: 8 for 8.30 pm
Carriages: 1 am

Please bring this invitation with you

- The name of the host.
- The name of the guest.
- The purpose of the party (if any).
- The date.
- The time.
- The place.
- The dress code.
- Food and drink provision.
And
- Name and address of the person to whom replies should be sent.

Mr & Mrs Suitable Guest

Liz Brewer

Requests the pleasure of your company

To celebrate her birthday
on Friday 6th June 2002
at
Annabel's, Berkeley Square, London W1

Regrets only:
21 Fantasy Road
London SW1
Tel. 020 0000 0000

Black Tie
Cocktails 7.00 pm
Dinner 8 pm
Carriages 1 am

A slightly less formal version of the standard invitation. (Once again, the name of the guest is handwritten.)

For security reasons, the wording 'Please bring this invitation with you' is sometimes included at the bottom of the invitation: it is not essential but it does help to check the gatecrashers.

Nowadays, with so much happening on the entertaining front, it is a good idea to send a 'reserve a date' card to forewarn guests of an impending invitation.

The 'reserve a date' card.

Mr Suitable Guest

Liz Brewer
Requests that you reserve the day
Saturday 7th September 2002
To celebrate the birthday of
Mr Mutual Acquaintance
In Monte Carlo

Formal invitation to follow

If you decide to take the more personal approach and telephone to invite people, it is still a good plan to send a written reminder – commonly known as a *pour memoir* – reiterating all the details. These are postcard size and can be sent as such. They do not normally require an RSVP as the guest will already have indicated their acceptance. For this reason, the telephone number is usually crossed out (though not omitted altogether in case the guest has any queries).

Mr Suitable Guest

Liz Brewer

Thanksgiving Lunch
Mosimann's Club
11b West Halkin Street
London SW1

Thursday 28th November

'Pour Memoir'
~~Tel. 020 0000 0000~~

Dress: Stars & Stripes!
12.30 for 1 pm

The *Pour Memoir*.

The Host
The most appropriate place for the host's name is at the top of whatever it is you choose to use for the invitation.

The Guest
The guest's name should be handwritten either in the top left-hand corner or on its own on a separate line, depending on the format and design of the invitation. You should also spell out whether you are asking the guest to come singly, or with his or her partner, or with an unnamed guest of his or her choice.

What or Who is the Party For?
Forewarn guests by stating clearly the reason for the celebration. If there is a 'guest of honour' this should be made clear. The idea of having a 'guest of honour' is the vogue in America and popular in Europe, and it gives an excellent excuse for having a party.

The Date

Include the day of the week as well as the date on the invitation. This makes it doubly clear when the party is and helps to cement the date in the guest's mind. I am sure this will ring some bells for you!

The Time

Bear in mind that very few people arrive at the time stipulated. Generally guests arrive fifteen to thirty minutes after the time indicated unless the host states 'From 8 pm' (or whatever), in which case the guest has greater discretion.

Always include the departure time if you do not want guests to overstay their welcome. If you do not wish to indicate a finishing time, be prepared for a mammoth 'sleep-over'! Something along the lines of the following gives a clear message of when the guest should depart:

Carriages

or Rickshaws,

Flying carpets,

Flying ducks,

Magic carpets,

Private jets,

or Walking shoes

Carriages (or Rickshaws, Flying carpets, Flying ducks, Magic carpets, Private jets, Walking shoes – or whatever else your imagination conjures up!) at midnight.

A helpful basic rule to consider is that drinks parties normally start any time between 5.30 pm and 7.30 pm and finish any time between 8.00 pm and 10.00 pm. If the finishing time is later than this it is not considered a drinks party and food ought to be provided (although a good host will remember that drinks parties need canapés or at least a little nourishment to soak up the drink).

Parties that include a main meal, whether buffet style or seated, if preceded by a reception, normally commence one to two hours before the meal is served. The wording 12.00 noon for 1.00 pm, or 8.00 pm for 8.30 pm, etc., generally indicates a seated meal and means precisely what it says.

If you want to be a stickler for time and make certain guests turn up promptly, show the hour – for example, '8.00 pm'; 'Carriages (or whatever) at midnight.

For brunch, the sky's the limit. But, generally speaking, 'from 11.30 am onwards' is the norm and quite often includes a few bubbles!

The Place

In addition to stating the name and address of the venue, either print a map on the reverse side of the invitation or enclose one on a separate sheet. Information on parking facilities is also helpful. Always add written directions – trust me, there are still people around incapable of reading a map!

Travel arrangements and accommodation

Give thought to those who may have to travel considerable distances to join you in celebrating. These people do you a great compliment by making the effort to attend and, in return, need consideration given to how they travel and where they might stay. Look into suitable hotel and B & B accommodation to suit all pockets. If you have friends who are able to put up guests over night or even give a house party, so much the better. List train services, taxi or good limousine services, car hire, and flight information.

Enclose good directions with your invitations to save your guests the frustration of ending up anywhere but at the party venue!

Whatever the venue, a chill in the air will make thinner bloods feel uncomfortable and unhappy. If the ambient temperature is likely to be cool, advise guests beforehand – either with an amusing addendum to the invitation (Dress: Black Tie and thermal underwear!) or in an accompanying note. Thermals can always be discarded during the evening, but there is nothing worse than feeling cold at a party. It induces frosty moods and matching memories of the occasion. The first time I stayed on the borders of Scotland at Ayton Castle – as a guest of David Liddell-Granger and Lady Christine de la Rue – fellow guests and I were shown the castle shop by Lady Christine and advised to stock up on thermals. At that time their heating system was in the process of being updated, and later at dinner I was thankful I had followed her advice. Aline Hay of Duns, whose castle on the borders of Scotland is wonderfully warm, nevertheless warns guests to bring thermals in winter – and she keeps a spare supply to give guests that arrive unprepared.

Dress

Convention dictates specific dress for certain occasions. A guide to such dress codes is given in Appendix 1. In general, when deciding on the dress code it is important to remember that clothes should suit the occasion and above all be comfortable and appropriate. A Black Tie, candle-lit picnic in the open air can be enchanting so long as the weather doesn't put a damper on it. Black Tie at a barn dance could prove awkward, uncomfortable and not so much fun.

When deciding a dress code, let your own personal preference be the main consideration. It is, after all, your party and you can dictate. Bear in mind, though, that a special occasion deserves a little more attention when it comes to dress. It is not every day you throw a significant party and so it is worth asking your guests to make a bit more of an effort. At a private function, as against a corporate event, you are the boss and you can allow your guests a certain amount of leverage. You may have noticed that nowadays there is a tendency towards preferring individual expression in dress to the conventional uniform type of dress. Frequently at Black Tie events you see men making a quiet statement in Nero jackets, black silk roll-neck shirts, or even designer black T-shirts with evening jacket. The name of the game is 'individual style' and, to my delight, men are at last adopting this in the way they dress, whether for the evening or otherwise.

Whatever you decide the dress code should be, it is important to make it clear on the invitation. (Usually it appears in the bottom right-hand corner.) Simply stating 'Evening dress' or 'Formal Evening Dress' is not good enough. It is better to be precise, otherwise you can expect tedious phone calls asking 'How formal?', 'Does that mean long or short?', 'White Tie or Black Tie?', and so on.

Suitable footwear

If the occasion takes place outdoors or on a boat, take care to warn guests concerning footwear. Correct footwear on board is 'shoeless' (in order to protect the decks), and shoes are normally removed as you set foot on board. More lenient owners allow rope or rubber soles, while on larger and more commercial boats used for banqueting purposes shoes are generally not a problem.

High heels are uncomfortable on grass and look out of place on a polo ground or on a lawn at a garden party. If you feel that the venue or the circumstances may create discomfort for wearers of high heels, suggest to guests that they bring a change of shoes.

If, as a guest, you are not sure what footwear would be most appropriate, take a shoe bag with a change of more practical, or more elegant, shoes – whichever is the case – so that you will have an alternative once you have assessed the situation. There is nothing worse than wearing shoes that hurt or are unsuitable.

INVITATION FORMAT AND DESIGN

There are no hard and fast rules on the size of an invitation. However, to be practical bear in mind that it is more economical – and simpler – to stick to the measurements that fit the standard-size envelopes. Formal invitations are generally 7 × 5 inches (18 × 12.5 cm) or 4 × 3 inches (10 × 7.5 cm) and are die cast; although this tradition is fast disappearing, I must admit I still pass my thumb over an invitation to check! 'At Home' cards, available from most stationers, are pre-printed and convenient to use for dinner parties and drinks or cocktail parties. If in any doubt about size or style, pop along to your local printer and look through his sample books.

Nowadays, with the wonders of modern technology, people have discovered the fun of creating and printing invitations on their own computers. Occasionally I have resorted to this method either from necessity through lack of funds (for example when organising a charity fundraiser), or through lack of time. In any case I often work out the format of an invitation on my computer before giving it to the printers as this cuts down on the cost of artwork. If you are having your in-vitations professionally printed, make sure you see a proof so that you

Front cover of the 1999 Cotswold Hunt Ball invitation.

Cartoon by Bernard Parkinson

can check that all details are correct before giving the printer the final go-ahead to print the required number.

Think Creatively

Designing invitations is a good opportunity to dream up interesting ideas. Experiment. If you have any kids around see if they come up with any bright suggestions. Children's minds have a freshness that gives them the knack of introducing spontaneity to a design. Otherwise get together with a friend and see if two minds can create better than one.

This is an invitation I used to celebrated Dame Shirley Bassey's sixtieth birthday and her host's fortieth. Note the 'Tenders at Midnight!' It worked, and no one fell overboard or for that matter had to be keel hauled!

Henrik Jönsson
requests the pleasure of your company
to a 'naughtycal' party to celebrate his and)

Shirley Bassey's
Joint 100th Birthday

on Saturday 10th May 1997
on board the
S/Y PENELOPE

anchored off The Carlton Hotel Pier, Cannes, South of France
(tenders will be operating every 10 minutes from 19.00 hours)

R.S.V.P. Shirley Bassey
c/o Liz Brewer
Tel: +44 171 730 7508
Fax: +44 171 730 5094

Dress: a touch naughtycal!
barefoot on board
Time: from 19.00 hours
last tenders at midnight

Please bring this invitation with you

If all else fails get your printer to recommend a good graphic designer. Explain what is required, get a quote, and pray for worthwhile results. One of the most memorable invitations I used years ago to celebrate the opening of Brian Stein's first Maxwell's in Covent Garden was an ingenious card, which contained a pop-up of the front of his restaurant. At that time launching hamburger bars was not my forte but, after many hours, Brian persuaded me. At four the following morning, not being able to sleep, I realised there was no way I could do it, so I wrote Brian a letter. I explained how guilty I would feel taking the high fee – which I would still charge – and that I thought early September was the wrong time and, above all, that I really didn't know this market. I hand-delivered the letter to his office at five o'clock in the morning only to be woken at eight by Brian returning my letter, telling me that I could not go back on my word. He charmingly assured me that it didn't matter if no one turned up – I had to do the party. So, convinced that most people would be on holiday, I trebled the guest list and went into overdrive. I even invited a few pearly kings and queens for good measure.

Then a miracle happened. Almost all those invited returned from holiday on the day of the opening, looking brown, feeling good, and in the party mood. Practically everyone turned up! How Brian coped I will never know but over 500 people were fed that evening. The only tragedy was that a couple of Bentleys and three Rolls Royces were towed away, including Marvin Gaye's car – the driver having gone off for a quick bite. It hit the headlines and suffice to say I don't think Brian ever looked back.

Caviar tin invitation, designed for W. G. White's centenary celebration and launch of Caviar Soup.

A misunderstood Invitation

When dreaming up innovative or unusual invitations, there is of course the risk that the joke may backfire. When I had the privilege of organising the centenary celebration for one of the world's leading suppliers of caviar, W. G. White, by launching Caviar Soup, I arranged a seated dinner for twenty-two celebrity guests at Mosimann's Dining Club in London's Belgravia. I sent out the invitations, which I had printed on my computer and embedded in empty tins of beluga caviar. Each individual invitation was rolled up in the form of a scroll, then tied with a blue satin ribbon, and laid on a bed of fake caviar created from tiny polystyrene balls normally used for packing cases. The Wessex Police did not appreciate this unusual idea. The entire local bomb squad was summoned in force to Longleat House; home of the Marquess of Bath, by a worried butler who assumed that his Lordship's invitation contained a bomb!

It felt like one, rattled like one, and – according to the police – it looked like one, and it was especially suspicious as Lord Bath had been expecting something of the kind from some political animal rights campaigners. I had to contend with an irate police officer who telephoned me demanding to know what I was up to. By coincidence, at that time, I had sent another 'missile' to the Marquess of Bath. This one, in a Wild West-style 'Warrant For The Arrest Of' format, was inviting him to the launch of a restaurant called the Texas Embassy Cantina. I assumed the police officer was referring to that invitation and so went to great lengths to explain it was not a real warrant, merely a spoof invitation, before realising we had our wires crossed. Anyway, I apologised profusely, assuring him that I had not meant to cause alarm. It had never occurred to me that my rather unusual invitation might be mistaken for a bomb.

Spur of the moment invitations

Sometimes, deciding to organise a spur of the moment soirée, I have really had to stretch my imagination. A private Christmas dinner party I hosted in honour of Dame Shirley Bassey, with one week's notice and seated for thirty, needed something striking and Christmassy fast.

It was whilst creating this invitation – in the shape of a cracker – that I discovered the magical qualities of sparkly coloured glues, which can be smothered with the tiny, shiny, metallic cut-outs that are easily available from most stationers. The only problem, I have to admit, was in the delivery of these invitations: owing to the shape of the cracker, they had to be boxed. Another year, I used the same idea with mistle-

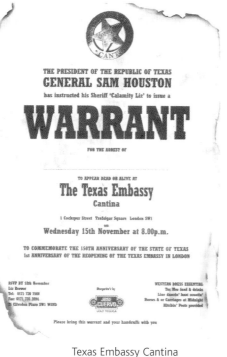

Texas Embassy Cantina invitation.

toe. They achieved an equally successful result while fitting more easily into a normal large envelope.

INVITATION DISPATCH AND REPLY

Having checked that the addresses, and especially the postcodes, are correct, post your invitations in good time. There are no strict rules dictating how far in advance of an event invitations should be sent, but the following is a guide.

■ Important events, such as weddings, special anniversaries or birthdays: six weeks ahead. (In some cases, especially for very important occasions, you can post up to three months in advance, although it is then advisable to follow up with a reminder call or card closer to the date – *see* page 28–9)
■ For charity events: one to two months with a reminder sent seven to ten days before.
■ Normal cocktail party: two to three weeks.
■ Dinner party: two to three weeks (unless spur of the moment and informal).

Telephone invitations are totally flexible, although the call is normally made one to two weeks in advance with a *pour memoir* sent to arrive two or three days before the event.

As you receive replies, immediately mark the acceptances and refusals on your main guest list. If the replies are written this is a good time to cross-check your address book to make certain that the address, post code, and various telephone, fax and e-mail numbers you have for that guest are correct and up to date.

Once you start to get a feeling for the numbers likely to attend, act swiftly to top up on guests if necessary.

FORMS OF ADDRESS

When writing and addressing invitations, make sure you use the correct name, spelling, and title of your potential guest. It is very irritating to receive an invitation with your name spelt wrongly and even more annoying when the title is incorrect. So make an effort to check. If in doubt ask – it will be appreciated. Correct forms of address usually depend on your degree of friendship. If your acquaintanceship is slight and you are not sure how someone is styled, consult *Whitaker's Almanack* or a copy of *Who's Who* and stick to the formal address. For a brief guide to formal styles of address, *see* Appendix 2.

'*Imagine all the people...*'

John Lennon
'Imagine'

branch 3

venue

Choice of venue is very much a personal decision that will be influenced by budget, number of people, convenience, and what would give you and your guests the most enjoyment. For most venues, initial contact for booking should be made through the appropriate authority – usually the banqueting manager, the manager, or the owner.

Availability can be a problem, so it is wise to book as far in advance as possible. If it proves impossible to book your favoured venue for the date you have in mind, do not give up – there are always alternatives. (A list of assorted venues for the reader to ponder and play with is given on page 40.)

Duns Castle, Berwickshire, the home of Alexander and Aline Hay of Duns.

Having selected a few desirable venues, and confirmed that they are available, you are ready to start looking into their viability and scope. Weigh up the pros and cons of each alternative. Take as many details as possible into consideration, and start doing a feasibility study and cost analysis. This is also the time to start bargaining with the various powers that be in order to get the most attractive deal.

POSSIBLE VENUES

Aeroplane/airport
Airship
Amusement park
Art gallery
Ballroom
Banqueting hall
Bar
Barge
Barn
Beach
Boat
Boat yard
Bus
Car park
Castle
Caves
Church hall
Cinema
College hall
Conservatory
Country club
Dance hall
Desert/desert island
Discotheque
Dungeons
Exhibition hall
Factory
Fairground
Farm
Ferry
Film studios

Flotilla
Forest
Garden
Garage
Harbour
Health spa
Hospital
Hot-air balloon
Hotel
Hot tub
Ice rink
In bed-slumber parties!
Lagoon
Lake
Lighthouse
Livery hall
Marquee
Members club
Mountains
Museum
Night club
Opera house
Palace
Park
Pier
Planetarium
Playground
Polo ground
Private house (yours or friend's)
Pub
Race course/track

Restaurant
Retirement home
Roof
Ruins
Safari camp
Sailing ship
School
Ship
Shop
Space station
Square
Stables
Stadium
Stately home
Station
Steam train
Street
Studio
Swimming pool
Temple
Tent
   (tepee/Arabian, etc.)
Theatre
Tower
Town hall
Train
Vineyard
Waxwork museum
Yacht
Yacht club
Zoo

NEIGHBOURS

Whenever you are celebrating at home or at a friend's house, it is polite to let the neighbours know, especially if they are not being invited. The last thing you want is complaints about noise or badly parked cars. Alerting them will at least give them warning and may help to diffuse annoyance, which might otherwise result in an unpleasant incident or unsympathetic or aggressive reaction. Frankly, if you are planning a large party it saves an awful lot of bother just to include the neighbours.

SAFETY AND SECURITY

One thing you will never regret paying particular attention to is security. Increased activity, with people coming and going, delivering and collecting, is an open invitation to thieves. One friend of mine, the morning after a fabulous party, gratefully let in a team to clear the contents of the marquee, including all the hired equipment, left-over supplies, hired crystal and china, and so on. They did a great job: nothing remained. Only problem was that half an hour after they left the real caterers arrived. To avoid such disasters it is well worth finding a capable person to take responsibility for the security before and after the event.

Strict security on the door is vital. Uninvited guests can be extremely annoying, and it is best to keep them – and any other undesirables – from entering. Much will depend on the event, but as a general rule this important job should be done by a reliable security firm or other person who is aware of the problems that may arise. The 'Corps of Commissionaires' do a grand job. They are fully uniformed and recruited from retired servicemen. They charge very little and deserve every penny!

Fire Precautions

You have a responsibility towards your guests to make certain safety precautions are taken, especially concerning fire. Fabric needs to be fire-proof. This includes marquee linings, tablecloths, chair covers, and all soft furnishings. Candles can easily fall and ignite fabric. Even light fittings can overheat and cause fire. Small household fire extinguishers should be at hand in every home. For a large event, especially, make certain they are readily available – and visible. Emergency exits should be clearly marked and easily accessible.

If they occur in your own home, accidents to your guests could be your responsibility, so check your insurance policies to see what is or is not covered.

Bear in mind that depending on the venue you are using you may also need to contact the local authority to check what precautions must be taken to comply with regulations (*see* Branch 1).

Informing Police

Depending on the number of guests, informing the police is sometimes not only a necessity but an advantage. Forewarned is forearmed, and in my experience if you work with the police with the right attitude they can be extremely helpful. Not so long ago a kind officer even drove a certain guest of mine home – the guest being rather the worse for wear. On several occasions, instead of towing away badly parked cars they took the trouble to allow us to announce the offending car number so the grateful owner could have the car moved.

All commercial establishments should hold public liability insurance, but it never hurts to double check. Whatever the occasion, be prepared for accidents. A first-aid kit should always be on hand along with the necessary contact numbers. You cannot always count on there being a doctor or nurse amongst the guests.

FACILITIES AND UTILITIES

Parking

When assessing a venue, take parking facilities into account. If you are expecting large numbers of guests to arrive by car, and your party venue does not have adequate parking, you will have to make alternative arrangements. One option is to employ the services of insured and experienced car jockeys (*see* page 112). Another is to find out where the nearest car park is situated and arrange for small mini buses to ferry guests to and from the venue.

If the numbers of cars expected are great then warn neighbouring establishments or homeowners to help prevent the inconvenience causing bad feeling. I remember the first charity event I organised way back in the 1970s. It was called The England Ball, held at Aubrey House (the home of Anka and Peter Dinely), adjacent to Holland Park. It was given to benefit the Council for The Protection of Rural England and presided over by the late Lord Henley. A few days before the event the local police informed me the event could not go ahead unless I organised sufficient car parking facilities. Fortunately I had an enthusiastic hard-working team of voluntary helpers who constructed an ingeniastic wooden bridge and tree walk. This led from the local school playground (and car park), over the boundary wall to connect with the grounds where the event was to be held. I was lucky the school authorities were so helpful, but for me it was a lesson well learned.

Dame Shirley Bassey and Liz Brewer celebrating Dame Shirley's 60th on SY *Penelope*, Cannes, south of France.

Loos

Lavatory, WC, bog, John, head, toilet if you must!, cloakroom, bathroom, washroom, powder room, Men/Women, Ladies/Gents … Whatever you wish to call them, they are a must. They should be well signed, and furnished with ample supplies of necessities, including lavatory paper, soap, tidy bin, tampons, and clean hand towels (paper towels are probably more hygienic unless you have a large supply of small towels and an attendant keeping an eye on things). If the venue does not have adequate loos, it is advisable to hire mobile ones, as used at most commercial open-air events. This can be organised either through the caterers or, if using a marquee, through their company or contacts.

It is also a good idea, especially if you are having 'fancy dress', to provide safety pins, needles and cotton, hairspray, and make-up.

Cloakroom

Weather being what it is, it is important to have facilities for coats, raincoats, umbrellas, galoshes, wellingtons and even snow boots.

If you are entertaining at home, you can clear a hanging cupboard for this purpose. If your party is to be held elsewhere, and the chosen venue has no facilities of this sort, you will need to improvise. The bare necessities are an attendant, dish for tips, coat rail, and ample supplies of hangers and cloakroom tickets. Obviously the more guests you have and the worse the weather the more equipment you will need. Clothes rails can be purchased or hired at a very reasonable cost and are easily dismantled for storing away; wire coat hangers are obtainable very cheaply from most hardware or chain stores. For cloakroom tickets use raffle tickets, which are available from most party shops.

Power
It is important to check that the venue has sufficient power to cope with whatever you have planned in the way of food and drink preparation and entertainment. Extra power may be needed for bands or discotheques, special-effect lighting, heating and air-conditioning equipment; and it may be necessary to hire a generator. Most performers have their own but you cannot count on this and should check the power output yourself as overloading the system can be dangerous.If in doubt, ask the professionals.

You also need to ensure there are sufficient power points, multiple points, and so on, and it is always a good idea to have extra adapters and extension leads available.

Air Conditioning
Although air-conditioning is rarely a necessity in the UK, there are occasional heat waves. To be too hot can be as unpleasant as being too cold. So if there is a chance the temperature may soar, and the venue has no air conditioning available, make certain you can hire or arrange for a portable unit or a sufficient number of effective fans for the occasion.

Heating
If guests are cold they will become very frosty, and this will be reflected in their memory of the occasion. If the venue is a marquee, large room or hall, make certain the area has been heated before guests arrive and that adequate heating is available during the event. If not, hire industrial heaters and arrange them so that they blast heat where it is required. These are available through marquee companies or the caterers.

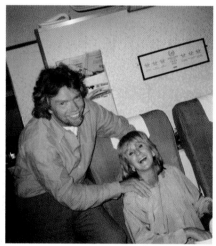

Sir Richard Branson and Liz Brewer partying on Virgin's inaugural flight to San Francisco.

Flooring

The ideal surface for dancing is wood. There is nothing worse than trying to dance on stone or carpet; and sand, although fun, is tiring! If your event is planned in the open or in a marquee then a portable, sprung wooden floor – which makes dancing a delight – can be hired through the marquee, discotheque or entertainment company. A portable oak-parquet dance floor, which generally comes in 3 × 3ft (90 × 90cm) sections, is fairly expensive but will make a noticeable difference to the enthusiasm that guests bring to dancing. Indoors, if there are no wooden floorboards to be accessed by rolling up the carpet, and a portable floor is not possible, then a sheet of cheap linoleum is a possible alternative.

If the venue has an existing ballroom, or other suitable surface, then the main factor to consider is whether there is sufficient space for entertainment and dancing. Squeezing too many energetic people into a small space may be cosy, but it's not much fun and can result in seriously damaged shins!

CATERING CONSIDERATIONS

Whether you are doing your own catering or bringing in professional caterers, the kitchen will be the main focus of work. Hotel and restaurant venues will of course have all the kitchen facilities necessary. If, however, your venue is a marquee or similar, or if the kitchen at the venue is inadequate or too remote from where the action will eventually take place, then you will probably need to hire at least some of the necessary equipment, which might include heating units and hot plates, portable ovens, or even a mobile kitchen. If you will not be using cold-storage units, you will need to allocate a small room or protected cool area that can be used for storing freshly prepared food. You may also need to set up a dispense bar. (*See* Branch 6.)

These factors, which will incur additional expense, should be taken into account when assessing the cost of using the venue.

Terence and Niki Cole dressed for the Rainforest party given by Peter and Polly Shalson to celebrate their marriage.

Be bold,
be brave…

branch 4

decor and theme

For a special event, fabulous and effective decor sets the party mood as soon as the guests arrive, igniting their enthusiasm and leaving a lasting impression. Therefore, it is well worth giving the decor careful thought and time. Whether this is achieved with the creative use of flowers and greenery, or taken to the extreme with a total transformation of the venue, will depend on your budget. If the budget allows, you may wish to bring in the professionals: this is an increasingly competitive field, and there are many up-and-coming specialists to choose from, so it is worth getting quotes from more than one. However, if expense is a consideration then you will need to rely on your own energy, enthu siasm and sense of creativity.

When strapped for cash and searching for inspiration and props for decor, I have struck lucky with thrift or charity shops, local interior designers offering me bales of unwanted fabric, the local theatre, who have let me loose in their props archives, and prominent department stores that on occasions have lent me an Aladdin's cave worth of

'The King' Richard Thirby at Lord Montagu's 70th birthday party.

window and other display material. When you put your mind to it there are no end of opportunities to beg, borrow, or barter.

HELP WITH DECOR

This is a must. If you are not bringing in the professionals then put an enthusiastic team of helpers together. Whether these are your kids, their friends, your friends, or whoever, it will surprise you how people love to be involved. Remember, though, to give credit where credit's due. People need to feel appreciated and sometimes in the thrill and speed of things we overlook people's feelings. With voluntary and unpaid helpers especially, make certain you notice their input, show your appreciation and mean it.

Luckily, I have a very eager team of serving officers from one of Her Majesty's regiments who love nothing better than to blow up my balloons. I also find them invaluable for heralding a special guest or the cake, or announcing dinner or a speaker. On one occasion, their reward was to meet the legendary star Dame Shirley Bassey (it was equally thrilling for her too!).

FLORAL DECORATION

Nothing beats the pure simplicity and effect of carefully selected and beautifully arranged fresh-cut flowers. There is so much talent and originality now in this field that decorating with flowers has developed into a whole new art form. I have seen and achieved exquisite and impressive displays using everything from cabbages to bales of hay. Gone are the days when symmetry dominated the floral show. Unusual effect and extensive use of the imagination is the vogue.

Some of the ideas I have used are:

Party at the Palace of Whitehall to celebrate Louis Vuitton's centenary.

■ Giant 'spider's webs' woven simply from wool or strong nylon thread, spanning white, silver or gold-sprayed branches of trees.

■ Fruit, vegetables and leaves, threaded securely with wire and wound around tent poles to disguise the poles and supplement other decorations.

■ Cascades of trailing greenery and pure-white flowers smothering balconies and banisters to give a breathtakingly romantic effect. (Simple but always a winner.)

■ Entwining flowers and greenery around tables, chair backs, doors, dance floors and windows.

■ Spraying leaves, nuts, fruit, dried flowers and twigs with gold and silver paint then wiring them in with the foliage. Leaves especially can be most effective when sprayed the colour of your theme and used profusely as camouflage or scattered over the tablecloth.

■ 12-inch (30-cm) inflated multi-coloured metallic jester masks (these and other designs are now available in the UK), with flowing streams of assorted ribbons, intertwined with long trailing bunches of greenery and wired together with fairy lights strung around the sides of marquee and tent poles.

Whether real or imitation, flowers can be enormously worthwhile. Mixing real and faux is an art, but satisfactory results are not too difficult to achieve. There are some excellent leaders in this field who can supply and advise you.

Flower Markets

Shopping in the flower markets in the early hours of the morning is an exhilarating experience and well worth the effort. Apart from the sight and smell of all the trees, plants and flowers, the atmosphere and jollity of the buyers and sellers – even at 4 o'clock in the morning – is infectious. At the 'New Covent Garden' market, Nine Elms, south of the Thames, there is a fascinating cross-section of early risers, from Ivana Trump, personally selecting her favourite orchids and white lillies, to Sophie and Michael Hanna, specialists in floral decor. Many times I

KEEPING FLOWERS FRESH

When using freshly cut flowers, adding an aspirin to the water will help to keep them looking fresh for hours longer. The sight of wilting flowers and greenery creates a sad impression. Keep them cool for as long as possible before the event, and if it is not possible to have them contained in water then wrap the stems with wet cotton wool or secure them in saturated blocks of foam or 'oasis' made specifically for this purpose. It is also possible to obtain small plastic holders for the stems of flowers or foliage; these can be filled with water and secured wherever they are required.

have used the Hannas' skilful artistry to transform the plainest of venues.

To buy flowers at a flower market you need to:

- Get up early.
- Pay the small entrance fee.
- Have a suitable vehicle in which to carry your purchases.

Florists' Materials

Creating spectacular and impressive floral displays is made easier if you use the proper tools and accessories. In addition to ribbon, wire and assorted foam-block bases for wet or dry arrangements (invaluable for table centres), florists' materials nowadays include numerous other items that can help you to achieve the result you want.

The suppliers of such materials are normally situated within the compound of the flower markets. At New Covent Garden, Nine Elms, they are around the edge of the market floor, where you can find everything you need for creating professional-looking arrangements. Good value are the 110-yard (100m) rolls of cheap but versatile florists' ribbon, which is available in every colour and width and can easily be split and coiled with tremendous effect. A little more extravagant and exotic, but still reasonably priced, are the rolls of wired ribbon. Foam block bases, available in a large selection of shapes and sizes, are a must when attempting table centres and other floral displays of specific shape. They are sold independently or by the dozen and are not expensive.

These outlets also have quantities of tempting bits and pieces to suit every occasion from important birthdays to Valentine parties and even new-baby celebrations.

Faking your foliage

Years ago, when I lived in Portugal's Algarve and sadly discovered I did not possess 'green fingers', I planted my entire garden on the cliff tops of Albufeira with plastic flowers. It caused alarm amongst the locals,

A Golden Girl: one of the 'decorations' at the Prize Guys Celebrity Auction.

and a huge amount of amusement to the ever-flowing number of guests who passed through my house, but it was better than a garden full of bare soil.

Things have progressed significantly since those days of plastic flowers. Fake is no longer frowned on, and there is now a wealth of subtle and realistic fake flora flooding the market. There are so many incredibly realistic reproductions of every type of flower and tree available that, bearing in mind that effect is what you are after, it could be your answer.

ICE

Ice Sculpture

Ice sculpture can be hugely effective and fun, and you can find specialists through most banqueting managers or even listed in the local directory. A professional ice sculptor can create whatever shape you require. As you can imagine, ice sculpture is time-consuming and an art form, so it does not come cheap. However, there are suppliers who use popular moulds, so request a brochure to see what can be provided and make certain the quote covers delivery and, if necessary, removal.

To launch the arrival in London of Avakian Jewellers, I transformed the first floor of the Carlton Tower Hotel into a Russian environment, completing the scene with ice sculptures of St Basil's Cathedral each side of the entrance. They were very impressive and very dignified. In contrast, and somewhat more exotic and popular, are the vodka luges carved in the shape of naked male or female torsos; and yes, the vodka does pour through the obvious orifice!

Dry-ice Machine

Dry-ice machines are easily available for hire, and they are great for creating a misty effect for the cabaret or for making much of the bringing in of a cake or the entrance of the guests to a dining area.

An ice scupture of St Basil's Cathedral.

However, it should be remembered that dry ice is in fact solid carbon dioxide, so it goes without saying that dry-ice machines need careful supervision, and they should not be overused as some people may react badly to them or may otherwise object.

BALLOONS

Now that balloons come in so many different sizes, colour, type and style, the only chore involved – once you have made your selection – is getting them inflated, tied, grouped and hung.

The impact value of balloons resides primarily in quantity: the more you use the greater the effect. As impact is what you wish to achieve, you cannot scrimp on numbers. If you decide, for budget reasons, not to use the services of a balloon company, you need to hire a gas cylinder and have at least two or three patient assistants to help you inflate and deal with the balloons. This takes careful planning as the life of a fully inflated balloon is limited. If they are to look fresh at the right time, the blowing up needs to be done a maximum of five or six hours before the event. It is advisable to inflate balloons as near as possible to the event's location as transporting them can be a challenging operation, especially with very large clusters.

If you are planning to place balloons outside, make certain that they stay out of the sunshine for as long as possible before the event. Balloons perish quickly in the sun, so if you want to prolong their lives position them in the shade (even if this is only temporarily until they are needed).

Entrance Indicators
Bunches of balloons are very helpful for indicating concealed entrances, and they are in any case an instantly recognisable sign of a party's location. When using this form of signing, make certain you have adequate security on the door as bunches of balloons can act as an open invitation to gatecrashers and other undesirables.

Balloon Sculpture

'Balloon sculpture' is an impressive way of creating a fantasia. I have seen life-size soldiers guarding entrances; arches leading to dance floors, numerous celebratory messages, and even a Mickey Mouse and Donald Duck – all formed from combining a mass of balloons. This is pure artistry and it needs a huge amount of patience, but there are people who specialise in producing these sculptures. Locate them through a party organiser or a party supplies shop.

One of the first people to supply and create 'balloon decor' was the Marquesa Nicole de Francisci, sadly now retired (the result perhaps of bursting one balloon too many?). She often came to my rescue and performed miracles with her skills. I am forever grateful to her for the night I was planning a special private birthday party at Annabel's nightclub in Berkeley Square for Ivana Trump. Seated for twenty-six, it was one of those last-minute arrangements and I had to put everything together in twenty-four hours. I realised too late on the evening that I had overlooked the balloons. Well, suffice to say that Nicole came up trumps. She opened the warehouse and produced 'He' and 'She' walking balloons – the first that the guests and I had ever seen. They were a huge success!

Balloons at Annabel's.

Netted for Release

One popular idea is to gather together a large quantity of balloons – a hundred minimum for the desired effect – in a fine net (available from a fishing tackle supplier). The net is then loosely secured with string and suspended from the ceiling. The string can then be withdrawn at an appropriate moment, freeing the balloons to float down over the dance floor or over the guests.

A Mass 'Float-off'

This is an interesting idea for a fundraiser, school/college party, club party, or for people who get together on a regular basis. Each person is given or (in the case of a fundraiser) buys a balloon to inflate. Each person's name is written on a stamped self-addressed card, along with the organiser's name and telephone number. The card, which also bears a message asking the finder to return it, or to inform the organiser where the balloon has landed, is then securely fastened to the knot of the balloon. At an agreed signal the balloons are released. The person whose balloon travels the furthest within a specified time wins the prize.

LIGHTING

Laser Beams
A knowledgeable lighting technician can create an incredible light show using lasers, and this can be an effective and terrific mood enhancer especially for a discotheque.

Fairy Lights
Tiny fairy lights give a wonderfully romantic or magical effect, especially when used in large quantities. Extension leads are usually necessary. Fairy lights can be twined around branches or added to the general decor and even, with the wires cleverly concealed, used to add sparkle to the table centre.

Floodlighting
If the budget can stretch to it, floodlighting the outside of the venue makes for a dramatic and memorable effect and helps put people in the party mood as they arrive. Once again, ask an electrician or lighting technician to set them up.

Torches and Flares
These are wonderful for lining a path or driveway or for creating an impressive effect at a front entrance. Flares, generally sold in boxes of fifty, are available from garden centres or in the barbecue section of department stores. Precise positioning will depend on the effect you wish to achieve, but placing them between 6 and 10 feet (1.8 and 3m) apart is a good guide. The average flare lasts about three hours.

Candles

The best way of buying candles is in bulk, either from a good discount outlet or from a market. I make the effort to be an early bird at New Covent Garden, Nine Elms. I enjoy the early morning experience and the friendly and helpful atmosphere, and there is a good selection of candles in the side shops around the edge of the market.

Do make sure you buy long-lasting non-drip candles. It is worth paying a little more as they will go much further and will not make a mess.

When placing candles, take care to ensure that they will not become fire hazards, and make certain they are firmly fixed into their holders.

Nightlights

Nightlights are fiddly but once lit and in place they give a brilliant party effect. When I am having a special evening at home I place them outside my front door and up each side of the steps. So long as they are in small glass containers (cheap small glasses are ideal), they will burn for hours and can be safely placed around a garden, along a balcony, on window ledges, or on tables or other surfaces around a room. If you wish you can add a few drops from an old bottle of perfume to the nightlights to enhance the setting with your own personal fragrance.

Candle holders

Virtually any appropriately sized container can be adapted to hold a candle or candles. The two most important points to remember are that the candles must be securely gripped or fixed to the holder and that there is something to collect the wax should the candles drip. In addition to melting the base of the candle I find using Blue Tac is good for fixing candles in place.

For flower arrangements, you can buy candle holders specially designed for use in florists' foam blocks, but these are not strictly necessary as I find that pushing the candle directly and firmly into the foam is usually sufficient.

Mimmi O'Connell at the Don Restaurant, London.

DEVELOPING A THEME

If you are using a theme, enjoy developing it from the beginning, starting with the invitations, which will stimulate the guests' imagination. Then follow it through to tie in with the decor, food, dress and indeed the entire event. Occasionally guests may even surprise you and take things a few steps further. I remember one such occasion when I had chosen an Adam and Eve theme. I leave the result to your imagination.

A cleverly thought out theme creates an impressive and memorable atmosphere and can be fun for all concerned, giving people a chance to add their own particular touch of creativity to the occasion. It is also a brilliant ice-breaker.

When choosing a theme it makes sense to match it to the reason for the celebration. Consider either something totally over the top and adventurous, or straight forward and simple. One of the most memorable parties great friends of mine gave to celebrate their wedding had a jungle theme. The invitation arrived hand-delivered in an impressive wooden box. The driver insisted the box be opened in his presence: once opened two butterflies flew out revealing the invitation nestling with another couple of fake butterflies. After such an invitation it was obvious things could only get more extravagant, which they most certainly did!

The first 'Prize Guys Celebrity Auction – Men for Sale' I organised to raise funds for seven leading cancer charities was attended by 300 of London's leading female dynamos. Filmed by Action Time – a television production company commissioned by ITV – the occasion had an evening theme of decadence, heavy glamour and romance. To enhance the atmosphere I had ordered 200 gold- and blue-metallic balloons, in the shape of celestial suns and moons, to swirl around the ceiling during the champagne reception, which was overseen by two gold-sprayed people portraying the gods Bacchus and Apollo. (I had also wanted a dozen blackamores waving fronds, but they were given the axe.) Imagine my surprise when, a week later, I arrived as a guest at an

The wedding invitation for the Shalsons' wedding.

Photograph: Jason Hurst

evening soirée given at the home of operatic producer and impresario Alan Sievewright and was greeted by a display of at least fifty of these same balloons. Totally relaxed and amused at my reaction, Alan explained how he, plus my gold gods, Bacchus and Apollo, had walked home carrying these huge bunches of balloons. He had found them easy to reinflate and use as an 'utterly divine addition' to his drawing room. I suppose I should have taken it as a compliment, but I have to admit I was somewhat taken aback!

Fancy Dress

Apart from adding to the colour of the occasion and being another brilliant 'ice-breaker', the real plus about fancy dress, costume or masquerade, is the opportunity it gives guests to cast off their inhibitions – sometimes to the extent that they end up playing the part suggested by the costume they are wearing. I'll never forget the fun I had, dressed appropriately in seven veils, for a '1001 Nights' theme party, when not a soul recognised me – the flirtatious character behind the yashmak.

Not every costume need be hired although this is certainly the easy way out. If you use your imagination and rummage amongst bric-a-brac and old clothes, never worn yet never discarded, it is amazing what you can create. At a masked ball held at the Albert Hall, my friend Tom Gilbey, the 'waistcoat king', turned up tapping a white stick, wearing dark glasses and a gondolier's hat, and with his head stuck through the slats of a large blind. What was he? Of course, a 'Venetian blind!' Sick, maybe, but a brilliant concoction and play on words.

At Lord Montagu's seventieth birthday bash at Beaulieu, guests were invited to come dressed to the theme, 'If music be the food of love – play on'. A challenge? Not, it appeared, for the few hundred who attended. There was everything from a human tiered cake smothered in plastic fruit to myself dressed in two short sheets back and front, pinned together and covered with musical notes cut out from black electrical tape. (Yes – I was 'sheet music'.) So you see how, with a little focused imagination, you can play with words and transform them into clever creations.

My sister, Victoria Watson, and my niece, Lucinda.

One sight that is never to be forgotten occurred at the annual fancy dress extravaganza given by leading social hostess Kookie Fallah. The theme was 'Anthony and Cleopatra' and a somewhat large guest appeared as an Egyptian mummy. She was completely bound in tight bandage from head to toe with tiny gaps for her eyes, nose, ears and mouth. Unable even to sit down, she certainly had guts and entered into the true spirit of the occasion. Her entrance was a knockout and is still remembered.

Masks, Props and Extras

There are always guests who are nervous of taking fancy dress too seriously. Fear of being 'the only one' and frightened of looking silly, they haven't the courage to participate, so they play safe. Then, on arriving to find that the majority of other guests have really made an effort, they feel somewhat left out and regret not having been more adventurous. A well-organised host will have a supply of assorted masks, scarves, hats or inventive headgear with which to deck out those who either couldn't be bothered or didn't dare to make an effort.

At one time I always took advantage of a trip to Rio, New York or Venice to visit party shops, especially at Hallowe'en or carnival time, to stock up with a selection from their overwhelming choice of masks and party props that were not then available in the UK. Now, however, there is an abundant supply – even through mail order.

Whatever you decide to include, there is always room to add your own personal touch. It can be enormous fun, as well as very rewarding, to get a group together, be they friends, family, kids or the local art college, to create the masks and props for a special occasion.

Make-up

In addition to the various props mentioned above, it is always a good idea to have a supply of easy-to-apply theatrical make-up and accessories for guests to use on their arrival. These should be set out in a well-indicated spare dressing room or bathroom. It is amazing how

Opposite: Richard Branson, Valerie Campbell, and Zandra Rhodes seated with 120 guests at Ivana Trump's engagement party at Syon House.
Photograph: Raymond Cooke

delighted and relieved those initially reluctant guests will be to join in the fun.

Professional face painting is another intriguing idea and always a major attraction at a party. Face painters can transform the entire face into a spectacular animal likeness or they can paint motifs, flowers or intricate patterns, or apply jewels.

The exotic non-permanent body art of the Far East is also becoming a favourite. Henna painting takes about fifteen minutes per guest, and the work is mainly done on the hands, upper arms or around the belly button. (Guests need to be warned that the henna does not wash off for at least seven to ten days.) A special henna powder and specific liquid ingredients are mixed to a dark paste. Using an applicator, linear designs are drawn on the body. Once it has set, the paste is removed to reveal reddish-brown markings on the skin; these gradually fade over the following days until they finally disappear. Although Madonna recently made henna artistry fashionable amongst the young in the West, it is nothing new. On the contrary, for over 5,000 years the people of India, Africa and the Middle East have practised the beautiful and mysterious art of painting on the body with preparations made from the henna plant. In India and in the West, the art is referred to as Mynd.

Musical toys

If you plan to put a musical accent on your party and want to encourage guests to join in the spirit of the occasion – especially during the dancing – supply an assortment of simple musical instruments. You can either scour toy shops for mouth organs, toy accordions, miniature trumpets, tambourines, and similar instruments, or you can visit ethnic shops, which usually have an assortment of pipes, rattles, simple drums or handcarved wooden whistles, and so on. Party-shop selections of cheap musical instruments tend to be of the paper whistle-blowing variety and not very exciting. I have found the most amusing and successful instruments to be the Mexican or Brazilian maracas, which

Stephen and Louise Kornfeld at a Hallowe'en Party at Duns Castle.

anyone with the slightest degree of rhythm can use effectively without causing irritation to others.

In Bali, at a party I attended near Ubud to celebrate New Year's Eve as guest of my sister and brother-in-law, Victoria and Ian Watson, we were all given a simple bamboo rattle just before midnight. Available in the local markets for a few cents, this rattle, called the Angklung, is based on the famous Balinese Gamelan ensemble of instruments, which are played at all the traditional dances and religious festivals and ceremonies in Bali. Each one is tuned according to its number, so:

1 = doh, 2 = ray, 3 = me, 4 = fah, 5 = soh, 6 = lah, 7 = te 8 = doh

We were then instructed to rattle our instruments in time with the numbers displayed on a large card. After a couple of attempts we mastered the rattles and with about a hundred other participants successfully played 'Auld Lang Syne' to perfection at midnight. You may think this infantile but I can assure you everyone thoroughly enjoyed themselves, including my young niece Lucinda, my daughter Tallulah, and an abundance of thirty- to eighty-year-olds!

'*After a good dinner one can forgive anybody, even one's own relations*'

Oscar Wilde
A Woman of No Importance

branch 5

the table

The size and shape of your table or tables will be determined by what is available at your chosen venue, or (if you are hiring tables and chairs separately) the size and shape of the location. In some cases, a number of circular tables seating six, eight, ten or twelve may be perfect; in others a series of trestle tables could be the ideal solution. If you lack the necessary serving tables, trestle or collapsible picnic tables are suitable alternatives. The most sensible way to determine your requirements is to make a floor plan, then, using cut-outs of table shapes, play around until you feel you have the right layout for the number of guests. (You could do this on your computer if you have the necessary software.)

TABLE LINEN

Tablecloths
Most colours and sizes of tablecloth are available (with matching table napkins) from catering companies to fit the different standard-sized,

circular, square, oval or long tables. All you have to do is select colour and size and agree the price. If for whatever reason you decide not to hire and not to instruct a catering company to provide what you require, you can use large old sheets as a uniform base over a silence cloth made from felt or green baize. Ideally these will cover the tables to the floor. If not, smaller ones can be tacked or pinned together and cut to fit, allowing for at least an inch (2.5cm) to flow onto the floor; if necessary the sheets can be hemmed to the correct length. These undercloths can then be hidden by an overcloth that will cover the top of the table in whatever dramatic colour or design of fabric you choose.

Some thought should be given to the choice of overcloth as it will influence the overall look of the table. Overcloths can be made from any number of different fabrics and materials to suit the theme or the mood you wish to create: theatrical, rustic, dramatic, elegant, humorous – anything you like. They can be cut from cheap material such as lining material, satin, mattress ticking, sacking, or nylon net (which is available from department stores in many different vibrant colours including gold and silver). When ordering the fabric remember to check whether it needs to be treated in order to make it fireproof.

For a professional banqueting effect, use a cloth just large enough to cover the top of each table. Then take a separate length of similar cloth whose width is equal to the height of the table (top to floor) and pin or slip-stitch it around the edge of the table, making small pleats or gathers every 6 inches (15cm) or so. The join can then be disguised using long swathes of fabric, broad ribbons or trailing leaves.

Overcloths are also very useful in helping to disguise a mishmash of unmatched tables. You can fit together an assortment of tables to make one long table and then cover them all with undercloths and well-matched overcloths to give a uniform appearance.

With a little time and thought you can include your linen in the theme. Experiment with potato cuts, wooden or rubber dye stamps, spray paints, or even coloured glues that expand, glow and glitter when dry. A client of mine, one of the largest growers of apples in the UK, was

length of fabric pinned around the table.

Using two pieces of fabric to make an undercloth.

celebrating his fiftieth birthday and was adamant that his party should have more than a flavour of the fruit. So I took on an extra couple of enthusiastic helpers and made potato cuts in the shape of apples. Then, using red and green fabric paint, we set about stamping the tablecloths. It took a little practice, patience, and a long clothes line for drying our finished work, but the results were terrific.

Table Napkins

Table napkins are primarily for protecting clothes and for wiping mouth and fingers. Paper napkins, which have crept into the catering arena, should whenever possible be kept for picnics and children's parties.

If you are following a theme through to the linen then an idea is to buy inexpensive napkins in bulk from a wholesalers or chain store and then add your own designs to them. Once, when my budget was minuscule, I laundered and starched some old cotton sheets then cut them into a hundred 12-inch (30cm) squares. Hemming was unnecessary: they looked extremely stylish tied with large strands of raffia.

The Banqueting Look

A table dressed to produce the banqueting effect.

65

Napkin holders or napkins folded?
This is a matter of personal preference. Frankly I am not a fan of fancy folded napkins – probably the result of having frequented too many hotel dining rooms! My preference is for a simply tied napkin. Many things can be used as the tie. Rope (ideal for a nautical theme), ribbons, raffia, supple twigs, strips of sacking, and even torn strips of brown paper. If you use your imagination you are bound to come up with something original. When tying the napkin, you may wish to tuck in a flower or even a name tag for the place setting,

When serving a buffet, one of the most sensible methods of dealing with napkins is to wrap them around the eating utensils. This way guests can collect all they require at the same time and will be less likely to drop things while finding a place to sit or stand and eat.

rolled into a wine glass

folded into a long glass.

Napkins rolled in wine glasses.

At a series of 'Breakfast At Tiffany' champagne breakfasts I hosted some years ago at Tiffany's in Old Bond Street, each guest's table napkin was secured by a bracelet of precious jewels. They had great fun comparing prices, which ranged from £5,000 to £150,000. Needless to say the bracelets were not allowed out of the dining room!

TABLE MATS

I am not a great one for using table mats with tablecloths although they are sometimes necessary to protect a good table top. While the choice of mat is really up to individual taste, size is important and should be relative to the amount of room allocated to each guest. If small mats are used, the cutlery can be placed either side of the mat rather than on it.

Mats are fun to include in the theme, especially if they are visible and not covered by a plate for the first course. Many years ago, for a special celebration for Arthur Anderson, I arranged for the mats to be created with a photograph of their London headquarters, as seen from the River Thames, with the dinner venue – a paddle boat – in the foreground. Needless to say most of the hundred guests took the mats as a memento, which was of course the idea.

TABLE DECORATIONS

When deciding on the table decorations, remember that guests need to see and be seen. They need to have eye contact. The golden rule is: keep table centres and decorations lower or higher than head height.

Impressive table decorations can be obtained with minimum effort but they nevertheless require a fair amount of forethought and attention. Don't be afraid to think theatrically. First impressions count, and an exquisitely and imaginatively decorated table will create a lasting sensation – as will any photographs!

Consider comfort and space when decorating the table. Bear in mind the amount of room available and be practical. Once the table is

tied with leaves

a half open quarter fold!

simply folded

Three ways to present a napkin.

laid with plates, cutlery, table napkins, glasses, name cards, salt and pepper, sauces, and perhaps ashtrays and bottles of water and wine, space will be at a premium. The sides are a good place for fixing trailing greenery, bows and the odd flower so long as they do not get in the way. It therefore makes sense to concentrate the main part of the decoration around or along the centre of the table.

Recently I did a couple of television programmes when I showed a simple method of making an impressive festive overcloth using plain gold net. Around the edge of the cloth, every 5 or 6 inches (13 or 15cm), I attached small bells, available from most haberdasheries. This can be done using tiny safety pins, short strips of gold wire, or simply by sewing. The cloth was then spread over the table and showered with tiny metallic stars; as a centrepiece, I used small glass containers of nightlights surrounded by clusters of gold-sprayed nuts and tangerines dusted with icing sugar to give a frosty effect.

Table Centres

The style of the table centre depends on the shape of the table. Long tables or large oval tables require long, low, trailing foliage, flowers and whatever appropriate extras you choose. Bear in mind though that flowers destined for a table centrepiece should not have an over-powering scent as this may interfere with the guests' enjoyment of the food. Sometimes a table requires more than one centrepiece. A good guide to follow is to set an arrangement in front of every third or fourth person. When more than one is required, you can fill in the gaps by extending trailing greenery between each arrangement. This can look very effective especially if it entwines the odd candle or nightlight.

For large round or square tables, height gives impact but this should be achieved without blocking the views of guests. This can be done in a variety of ways:

■ Use a very tall single-stemmed candelabra, with the main decoration, including items in keeping with the theme, flowing out from around the base and perhaps extending to trail up and around the holder. At the base of the candles at the top of the candelabra, flowers or foliage can then be arranged by setting them in soaked block foam (having first pushed the candles through the block to position them firmly).

▪ Take large, round, foam-filled bases (*see* Branch 4) and use them to secure spectacular arrangements to which you could attach gas-filled balloons. The balloons should be suspended on ribbons a minimum of 3 feet (1m) high. However, balloons do not mix with candles; better to stick to nightlights.

▪ Use tall (18–20 inch/45–50cm), slim, glass vases, but make certain the arrangement is not top heavy. These can be most effective filled with white sprayed twigs or small light branches and hung with small items to tie in with the theme.

Candelabras

In my opinion a classic silver candelabra is the most elegant and romantic form of lighting. These can be hired from the caterers, and some establishments supply them automatically.

There are cheap plastic versions, which can be bought from party shops and flower markets. If you are considering using these I would suggest you cover them dramatically and extensively with greenery so that only a glimpse of silver twinkles through. A few strands of ivy or any other available trailing slim pliable branches should work effectively, and you can always wire a few flowers around the stems to give an even more professional effect. Unless you are in a minimalist mood think drama and go with the flow.

PLACE CARDS

Once you have ascertained the names of the guests attending, you can start either handwriting or printing their names on place cards. Whether or not you use the guest's full name and title will depend on the tone and formality of the occasion. The important point is to ensure that you are consistent: do not write Mrs John Smith on one place card and Joan on the next one. Titled guests should be styled socially, i.e., Lord Somewhere, not The Earl of Somewhere.

Stationers and printers have selections of standard-sized cards ready for use, but there is nothing to stop you making your own, especially if you wish to slip away from the normal design and use your own ideas. This can be easily done on the computer or you can cut out 3 × 2½-inch (7.5 × 6cm) sections from sheets of quality paper, fold them in half, and write the guest's name on one side. There are various other ideas to explore, and I have used the following alternatives with success:

■ Toy tin soldiers carrying the guest's name on a simple small card attached to the arm.
■ Fresh leaves with the name written boldly in gold or silver felt-tip pen.
■ Torn brown paper, tucked into the napkin tie, with guest's name written in ink.
■ Card or other tag tucked into the cut side of an apple or similar fruit.
■ Menu cards with the guest's name handwritten at the top.
■ Gas-filled balloons with each guest's name handwritten with large felt-tip pen. The balloons can then be secured to the back of the individual's chair, preferably using long slim strands of ribbon.

Remember at this stage to keep an ample supply of extra place cards, or whatever you have chosen for this purpose, as many changes can take place with your guest list between the time guests accept and the time they actually arrive.

Calligraphy

If you decide to stick to using conventional place cards but think your handwriting is not up to scratch, find a good calligrapher to assist you. There will of course be a charge for the job (usually according to the number of names), but the effect is impressive and shows style.

MENU CARDS

Menu cards are another personal touch showing a degree of thought and attention to detail. Once the menu is decided these can either be printed on the computer or carefully handwritten by you, a helper, or an expert calligrapher. One idea is to allow menu cards to double as place cards, with each guest's name written on his or her personal copy of the menu.

With any important occasion the menu card is an ideal place to state the name of the host or hosts, and the date and reason for the celebration. Guests often like to keep the menu card as a memento.

TABLE GIFTS

However small or insignificant, an attractively wrapped table gift is a touching way of welcoming your guests to the table. Irrespective of the content they will be gratefully received and, I can assure you, taken home and often kept. I have seen 'superstars' seriously upset at the end of the evening upon discovering that their wee gift has 'walked'.

As to your choice of gift, there are so many promotions nowadays, especially in the cosmetic and fragrance world, that it is always worth contacting company PRs to see if any special promotions are being planned. Small musical instruments (*see* page 60) are always fun and an ideal way of encouraging guests to participate. A buttonhole for the men and corsage for the women is another attractive idea.

Gift-wrapping
Whatever you conjure up for gifts don't overlook the wrapping. As echoed in every aspect of the party, the all-important word presentation is what really counts. Consider new original ways of wrapping. This can be done using cellophane, fabric, wallpaper (very easy and effective), ribbons, and even leaves. Once, at a dinner in Indonesia, I received an interesting table gift wrapped in a banana leaf.

TABLE PLAN

As the host it is up to you to decide on the seating plan. You do, after all, know your guests (or at least most of them) and therefore know

CHANGING PLACE CARDS

Guests' changing the seating arrangement is of course a cardinal sin. To peek at the table settings before dinner and swap the place cards around is not only annoying for the host, who presumably has deliberately sorted out the placement according to their liking, but can be *very* embarrassing for the guest or guests if they are caught out. If a guest has a problem with the seating he or she should quietly explain to the host and let the host rectify the situation.

their preferences. So treat this challenge with the right attitude and you will find it can be fascinating, like doing a large puzzle. I have to admit I rather enjoy this part of the planning.

The simplest way to tackle the task is to take the prepared place cards and then sort them into groups representing tables. Arrange them so that each table will have someone who you feel will hold the table together. Thoroughly mix, match and swap around the names until you can almost hear the conversations that could be the outcome of your groupings. This done, use a pencil to mark the back of each place card with the number of the table and the seat (e.g. Table 1 seat 1, and so on) until you have accounted for all the place cards. You are then ready to either handwrite or type the main table plan accordingly. Obviously this operation is much simpler done on the computer.

If you find your numbers are not balancing it is time to consult your guest lists again.

Table Names and Numbers

If you have more than three or four tables, table numbers or table names really do help people to locate their places and are in any case necessary for a table plan. Your caterer or the banqueting manager at the venue will normally supply table numbers on request. But if circumstance requires you to provide your own this is an easy task – you can either make them yourself or buy them ready made and slot them into tall holders stuck into the table centres (available from florists or the flower market).

Table names are an interesting alternative to numbers, especially when there is a theme. For example, if 'Carnival' is the theme, table names could include 'Clowns', 'Mardi Gras', 'Masks' 'Musicians', 'Rio', and so on. To take this a step further, the table centres can be designed to reflect the name – the centrepiece of the masks table, for example, could sport a bizarre assortment of crazy Venetian carnival masks.

Many years ago, Elcin, a friend of mine and the widow of the former Turkish Ambassador in London, Gumru Cuagalu, used to give splendid dinner parties for around a hundred guests. When you arrived and entered the main salon for drinks before dinner, each guest had to pick a card from one of two baskets. One basket had a pink bow and was for the women, the other, which had a blue bow, was for the men. Each card had an illustration of, or was attached to, a flower. When it came to being seated for dinner you had to find the table whose centrepiece was a display of the flower on your place card – a very clever idea. It saves a great deal of time and effort with arranging precise placements, but of course you have no control over who sits next to whom. Sometimes good, sometimes not so good! I do remember Ned Ryan (a fellow wheatgrass-enthusiast friend of mine), and myself seriously cheating.

I'll never forget one particular charity ball at the Grosvenor House hotel in London. The dress was 'Goldfinger' and Dame Shirley Bassey had agreed to sing the famous theme song. Tickets were naturally in demand. Owing to some muddle in the organiser's office, my tickets were not forthcoming. When they finally arrived approximately three hours before the ball began, I remember mentioning to Shirley – who was rehearsing in the ballroom during the afternoon – that I was sure our table for twelve would be situated in the equivalent of Siberia. Sure enough, before we arrived at the ball, we learnt that it certainly was. What happened between the time of that conversation and our arrival we shall never know, but somehow the table numbers were switched. Unfortunately – and to my amzement – the well-meaning gesture resulted in our acquiring the top table! As our group was dressed in over-the-top Bond style (our table included some of Shirley's personal friends including Nabila Khashoggi, who was flying in specially for the occasion and even had a helicopter in her hair), I decided the best plan to avoid a major confrontation was to adopt a little Bond sangfroid, sit down and start dinner immediately. This we did, ignoring a table being rolled into the centre of the room, and outraged guests originally destined for the top table making their feelings apparent in no uncertain terms.

CHAIRS

Tables that are too high for the chairs or vice versa are anathema to me. To sit comfortably I like to feel I can (if I wish) put my elbows on the table with ease. I have lost track of the number of establishments where I have either had to ask for a cushion or sit on my coat! So if you are hiring tables and chairs, check this out before deciding.

The design and condition of chairs is too often overlooked, and yet they can do much to enhance or detract from the overall setting: the sight of a beautifully laid dining room whether for ten, a hundred or even a thousand guests, is so easily marred by unsightly chairs. Depending on the supplier's selection and your budget, chairs might be wooden, plastic, the small gold banqueting variety, foldaway or stackable, with or without armrests. If you are working with a tight budget and feel that the chairs you have available are unappealing, the solution is to give them a new stylish or romantic look using covers. This is especially successful when the chairs are of the banqueting variety – even the most obnoxious plastic chair can be Cinderellas for the night.

Whether you hire chair covers through the caterers (sensible for large numbers) or, for virtually the same cost but more effort, 'do it yourself', is up to you. The transformation is worth the work or cost involved. If you wish to mix an assortment of perhaps dining, garden, kitchen and whatever other chairs you have laid your hands on, they can all be disguised using lengths of cloth.

LAYING THE TABLE

Many rules were drawn up by past generations when entertaining was done with great style and an abundance of staff. It was then a way of life and such things were taken very seriously. Today, the approach to laying tables is very much more relaxed, although this does not mean that your table should be laid in an inelegant or slapdash manner (unless of course you are planning a 'bad taste' theme party).

Covering a chair.
Lay a length of cloth over the chair and secure with a large bow, tied at seat level to the rear. If the chair has arms, more fabric will be necessary, and slits will need to be made though the sides of the fabric at the corners of the rear base of the seat to thread ties around to the back to keep the fabric in place.

Often the quality and choice of crockery, cutlery and glassware is relative to the quality of caterer or venue chosen. If you wish to inject your own style, especially when dealing with low numbers, then this is an area in which you can be creative, resourceful and show some flair. But some forethought and planning are needed.

When entertaining small numbers never worry about not having sufficient settings of, say, your best dinner service. There is nothing wrong with mixing but try to do it with some style. Before now I have:

- Arranged each place setting with a different style of crockery, cutlery and glasses.
- Used two styles of everything, alternating the place settings.
- Organised a seated dinner at home for twelve using the place settings of a dozen well-known London restaurants (whose owners, I would add, kindly supplied these!).
- Bought an entire plain white dinner service and range of glasses from an auction house selling off the contents of a small hotel at bargain prices. I then painted all the plates in keeping with my theme, which was a twenty-first birthday celebration, and wrote the name of each guest on the glasses. The whole cost came to less than it would have done to hire, and I had exactly what was wanted for the occasion.
- Borrowed!

When deciding what crockery and cutlery to use, write down your menu, remembering also to take into account what will be served at the reception. So if canapés are being offered these will require serving dishes or trays. The equipment and utensils must suit the food being served. The lists given in the box on page 76 are a guide to what you might need, but when in doubt, ask! There is a wealth of people around who would be delighted to help you – the manager of a local restaurant, perhaps, or the banqueting manager of a hotel, or the director of a catering company.

Normally the wine merchant supplying the drink – spirits, wines, soft drinks, water, sodas, and so on, will 'throw in' the glasses on a complimentary basis. However, remember when hiring or borrowing glasses, and other items, to keep the container boxes in a convenient place. It is also sensible to clean the items and return them to their relevant boxes as soon as possible after use so that you can keep track of everything.

equipment and utensils

Cutlery

First course: small fork, or small knife and fork.

Soup: soup spoon.

Main course: large knife and fork. (A sharp knife will be needed if game or steak are to be served.)

Salad: small fork.

Cheese: small knife.

Pudding: teaspoon, or dessert spoon and fork.

Coffee or tea: coffee/teaspoon.

Butter: small knife.

(Caviar requires either licking from your left wrist – believe it or not the correct procedure! – or tiny mother of pearl or bone spoons, or a small knife and fork if served with blinis.)

Crockery

Bread or side plate: 7 inches (18cm) or smaller.

First course: plate, 10 inches (25cm) or smaller.

Soup: soup bowl, with or without handles, or suitable cup.

Main course: plate, 12 inches (30cm) or larger; round, square or oblong.

Salad: side dish or small plate.

Pudding: dish/bowl or suitable container.

Cheese: plate.

Coffee or tea: cup and saucer.

Fingerbowl.

Serving dishes: these need to be large enough to contain the food and light enough to be either carried or passed round. Lids help keep the food hot but can be cumbersome during serving.

Glassware

On guests' arrival:

Champagne, wine, cocktail, spirit or water glass, depending on what is being served.

During a meal:

Shot glass if serving vodka (with caviar) or whisky (with haggis perhaps!).

Small wine goblet for white wine.

Larger wine goblet for red wine.

Water glass.

Small wine glass for Port.

Brandy glass.

Liqueur glass.

A Conventional Place Setting

The following is a simple guide to what is generally done when laying a table, which in practice makes life easier for the host, for those serving, and for those enjoying the meal. However as I have frequently said, there is no one up there telling us souls down here, 'Thou shalt not stray from these guidelines!' There is nothing wrong with using a standard wine glass throughout a meal. And if you wish to serve your salad on a palm leaf in a bed of ice on a saucer, or your fish 'n' chips in paper – fine! Food needs to look inviting, and as long as the preparation and presentation are scrupulously hygienic, you can be inventive.

Cutlery

Having selected cutlery according to the menu, start laying it in the order that it will be used, working from the outside in so that cutlery for the first course is furthest from the plate. It is wise not to vary this as most guests will know to start from the outside and work inwards.

The knives and forks should be placed at right angles to the edge of the table, a large plate size (approximately 12in/30cm) apart and about an inch (2.5cm) from the table edge to reduce the risk of their falling off on to the floor. Knives should have the blades turned inwards; forks should have tines turned upwards. The butter knife can be placed either on the side plate or on the right adjacent to the inside (occasionally the outside) of the place setting

If soup is being served, place the soup spoon to the right of the knife that will be used for the following course.

Lay the forks and spoons for pudding above the place setting, or 'cover' as it is sometimes known, parallel to each other with the spoon above, its handle to the right, and the fork beneath with its handle to the left. More formally they can be treated in the same way as the other cutlery and placed either side of the cover (spoon right, fork left), to the inside of the cutlery that will be used for the preceding course.

At one time different types of fork were used for different types of food. For example, the fork used for hors d'oeuvres was different from those used for fish, meat, salad and pudding. Today, the difference in forks is usually in size not style. Generally, and whenever possible, a fork is used in preference to a spoon.

Crockery

It is a good idea to have a service plate in the centre of the cover ready to take whatever is the first course. This is particularly convenient with soup as it provides a resting-place for the spoon.

A small side plate should be placed on the left-hand side of the cover. This is for the bread, possibly the table napkin, salad or separate vegetables, and if left empty it is useful for anything else you may wish to remove from your main plate. So if you or your guests do find the

Floral centerpiece for a wedding dinner in Napa Valley.
Photograph: Michelle Pattee

odd fly in the soup, it can be discreetly transferred to the side plate without causing too much fuss! If fingerbowls will be necessary, they should be placed to the left of the cover above the cutlery.

Butter dishes or plates, sauce boats, ashtrays (fortunately becoming rarer), and any similar items that are to be used by more than one guest should be added at the appropriate time and placed where they can be most easily reached or passed round by the guests.

Glasses

The first glass to be used and the glass for water should be placed closest to the top of the right-hand side of the plate or above the tips of the knives, either grouped or in a line – whichever suits the arrangement of your table. If port or liqueurs are being offered, the glasses for these are usually placed on the table when the port or liqueur is being served, by which time most of the glasses except the water will have been cleared away.

Table napkin

This can be placed on the side plate, in the centre of the place setting (possibly on the service plate) or in one of the wine glasses.

Salt and pepper

Individual salts and pepper are placed either at convenient places along the centre of the table or, if in ample supply, to the left of each cover.

'Eat, drink, and love; the rest's not worth a fillip'

Lord Byron
Sardanapalus

branch 6

catering

The catering equipment that you will need will be largely dictated by the venue's existing facilities (if any) – *see* Branch 3. Determine your requirements at an early stage in the planning so that you can be sure of obtaining – by purchase or hire – whatever is necessary.

If food is to be prepared in advance on the premises, some items of food and drink may need to be kept cool, either in cold-storage units or in a small room that can be used solely for the purpose. To assist in keeping the temperature low, you can use this space for storing ice or blocks of ice (although you will need to place them either in large containers or in bin bags to avoid a flood!) A closed bathroom with ice blocks placed in the empty bath is ideal, especially if you cover the bath with large trays, or a piece of cheap plywood on which to place the food.

The golden rule when serving hot food is that it should be hot! If the kitchens, ovens, vans or whatever are providing hot food are situated a 'cooling distance' from the dining area then you will need hot plates or heating units set up as near this area as possible. Food for large numbers

Patsy Baker, Christopher Buxton and Liz Brewer at Royal Ascot.

81

is especially prone to becoming cold so the heating equipment must be adequate and suitable for the location and the numbers being served. In some cases, it may even be necessary to hire a mobile kitchen.

Plan your menu well in advance. It is a good idea to prepare a tasting for yourself with a discerning friend, inviting creative criticism. Apart from finding out how the dishes taste and work together, it will also give you a chance to practise the co-ordination and preparation of the food and to decide how much is required. Draft an action timetable for yourself listing the items that can be bought and prepared in advance and those that need to be prepared at the last minute. Fresh food requires careful buying and planning with maximum focus on keeping the dishes fresh once prepared. (This is where a plentiful supply of airtight containers and cold storage facilities will prove invaluable.)

SUPPLIERS

Choose your food and drinks suppliers carefully. Suppliers are experienced professionals who will be able to provide you with a wealth of advice and assistance, so it is worth going to the trouble of finding a good one. When dealing with suppliers, it is important to:

- Take time to build a good relationship.
- Explain what you require, and be explicit.
- Be definite about your budget.
- Ask advice, and heed it – it is all part of the service.
- Study their terms (see Branch 1).

MENUS

If you are in doubt about putting together a suitable menu, consult a good cookery book or ask a friendly chef.. You could even telephone a few suitable caterers or restaurants and ask them to fax you a copy of their menus, which you could then use for inspiration.

Aline Hay of Duns as a guest of Ivana Trump at a crab bake in Florida.

Whilst a full guide to menus is beyond the scope of this book, I have included some suggestions for canapés and buffets. These are intended to be used only as a guide. For a special event most caterers can offer themed and specialist canapés. Serving canapés on trays can be most effective, especially when the trays are lined with large fresh green leaves or colourful and even edible flowers such as nasturtiums. The menus for hot and cold buffets were kindly recommended to me by Joanna Towler of Table Talk.

Canapés (Served Hot)

Fish

Monkfish tempura wrapped in nori and sweet and sour dipping sauce
Shrimp in crisp beer batter with mushy peas as dip
Thai fishcakes with a chilli dip
Fish and chips served with ketchup, salt and malt vinegar in *Financial Times* cones
Tiny smoked haddock and prawn fishcakes with a greviche dip
Spiced crusted salmon with a honey and miso dip
Crab and sweetcorn fritters with a sweet chilli dip
Smoked fish and sweet potato cake with Cumberland crème fraiche

Meat

Crispy chicken with teriyaki dipping sauce
Peppered fillet of beef with a Béarnaise dip
Sweet belly pork in a tortilla wrap with apricot salsa
Chicken and mango spring roll with sweet chilli dip
Sizzling venison sausages with tamarind dip
Chorizo and smoked mozzarella empanadas with a spicy tomato dip
Salt beef and caramelised onion dumplings with Piccalilli
Spiced lamb koftas with a sweet mint dip or sour cream
Lamb skewers with a yogurt and peanut dip
Chargrilled pork and prawn dumplings

HOW MANY CANAPÉS?

If you are not sure how many canapés you will need, the following is a guide:

For a reception lasting 1–2 hours: 6–8 canapés per person.
For a reception lasting 2–3 hours: 10–12 canapés per person.

For a reception lasting any longer than this, more substantial finger foods should be provided.

Quail's egg benedict – poached quail's egg on a toasted muffin with smoked ham and hollandaise sauce

Mini crumpets with melting mozzarella and Parma ham

Vegetarian

Tempura – Japanese deep-fried vegetables with a teriyaki dipping sauce

Mini crumpets with melting mozzarella and chargrilled courgettes

Pumpkin and sage risotto balls with smoked tomato sambal

Thai spring rolls with ginger and coriander and a hot chilli dip

Spring onion and mango pakora with mint raita

Beignets with roasted garlic and wild mushrooms

Mediterranean vegetable cigarelle

Vegetable wontons with a soy and ginger dip

Canapés (Served Cold)

Fish

Thanksgiving lunch served at the Optimum Health Institute launch in Austin, Texas.

Lobster on a lemon croûte with aïoli mayonnaise and rocket

Seared five-spice tuna, with pickled carrot on a crisp noodle cake

Lime-marinated tiger prawns with a coriander hollandaise

Potted wild salmon on granary bread with kumquat and mustardseed marmalade

A selection of sushi

Red mullet and home-dried tomatoes on a basil croûte with pesto

Branade of salt cod crostini with piquille pepper

Seared scallop on a crispy buckwheat noodle cake with galangal cream

Meat

Smoked seared pork fillet with tamarille chutney

Chicken and choi sum rolls (maximum 100 guests)

Chicken tikka on a plantain crisp with cucumber raita

Carpaccio of beef on olive oil croûte with shavings of Parmesan, rocket and truffle oil

Rare fillet of lamb on crostini with a piperade salsa
Charred bruschetta with proscuitto crudo and a fig and onion marmalade
Crispy quail with pomegranate chutney on toasted brioche
Spiced duck and cashew nuts in filo with a sweet plum sauce

Vegetarian

Caramelised baby onion tartlets with thyme
Pumpkin shortbread with succotash and stilton
Tomato and onion twisted Swiss cheese straws
Crostini of creamed beans and deep-fried sage
A shot of watercress soup, with a light cream froth
Lemon and coriander marinated artichoke on a thin Parmesan croûte drizzled
  with olive oil
Caponata in a Parmesan wafer
Watermelon and feta skewers with pumpkin seeds
Marinated feta with figs, olives, fresh mint and balsamic dressing

Hot Buffets

Fish

Salmon fishcakes with spicy tzatziki and baby spinach leaves
Smoked fish pie topped with a creamy chive mash
Seared salmon with sugar snaps, spring onion and bok choy
Salt and chilli squid with puy lentils and rocket and roast vine tomatoes
Skewered squid and tiger prawns, with sweet chilli, coriander and lime
Clam and tomato risotto topped with fresh herbs
Grilled tiger prawns with a quinoa, coriander and mint salad and a green chilli
  and yogurt dip

Meat

Lamb tagine with prunes and minted yogurt
Boeuf bourguignon

Chargrilled chicken with butternut squash, confit red onions and roasted pepper
Crispy duck on fermented black beans, bok choy and chilli
Frittata, chorizo, red pepper, potato and goat's cheese

Vegetarian

Pappadella, lemon buerre blanc, broad beans, tomato and fresh mint
Porcini risotto with Parmesan shavings and truffle oil and rocket
Teriyaki braised aubergines, crispy noodles and smoked tomato sambal

Salads

Chicken caesar salad
Antipasti (Parma ham, coppa, bresola, olive and sun blushed tomatoes)
Puy lentils with bacon, roast shallots and wilted spinach
Crushed Jersey potatoes roasted with rosemary and garlic horseradish mash
Root vegetable purée drizzled with crème fraiche
Wok seared yaki-sobi noodles, oriental vegetables and bok choy
Beans and peas in their pods
Chick pea and tahini mash

Puddings

Apple tarts fines with honey ice-cream
Lime and praline cheesecake
Tarte au citron
Warm lime-cured soufflé with mango sorbet
Banana risotto with caramelised banana
Dark bitter chocolate tart with mandarin sorbet
Blueberry and vinsanto jelly with a champagne sabayon

Cold Buffets

Fish

Tuna niçoise with quail's eggs, French beans, vine tomatoes, new potatoes, olives and anchovies

Jeannette Norell's garden lunch for my special friend Louie King from Texas.

Salt cod, chickpea and Swiss chard salad with potatoes, peppers and a lemon
   olive-oil dressing
Lobster salad with new potatoes and cornichamps dressing
Salted squid with puy lentils, rocket and crispy shallots
Skewered tiger prawns with a quinoa, coriander and mint salad and a green chilli
   and yogurt dressing
Seared salmon, with sugar snaps, mizuno leaves and sweet-pepper dressing
Buckwheat noodles, wakame, baby scallops, spring onion and ginger salad
Tiger prawns, new potatoes, chorizo and rocket salad with aïoli
Swordfish and salmon carpaccio, rustic guacamole with sweet chilli
Roast salmon fillet, chargrilled asparagus and a soft-boiled egg

Meat

Salt beef with a wasabi sauerkraut and a homemade Piccalilli
Vitelo tonnoto – thinly sliced veal fillet with a fresh tuna and lemon sauce
   and capers
Crispy quail, roast pumpkin, pine nut and pomegranate salsa
Sweet belly pork on qhite bean and sage salad with red pesto
Confit duck salad with snake beans and yaki soba noodles
Schwain beef with red peppers, beansprouts and mange tout
Chargrilled chicken with spiced red lentils and baby spinach leaves
Chargrilled chicken with baby gem lettuce, peas, baby artichoke and roast vine
   tomatoes and pesto
Smoked chicken salad with avocado, walnut and pancetta
Spicy lamb with a tangy tomato sambal, roast aubergine and caramelised
   baby onions

Vegetarian

Couscous with roasted tomatoes, peppers and goat's cheese
Three-bean primavera with olives, home-dried tomatoes, capers, olives and
   salsa verde
Watermelon, pumpkin seed and feta salad
Chargrilled vegetables, baby artichokes, endive, walnuts with brioche croutons

A centrepiece of prawns at
Sarastro restaurant, Drury
Lane, London.

Roast baby aubergine marinated in teriyaki sauce, served with pickled carrots and garnished with mizuna leaves
Red onion and Gorgonzola tart
Marinated baby artichokes, chargrilled new potatoes, and crispy red onion on wholemeal bruschetta

Salads
Tomato and basil salad with olive croutons
Little leaf salad
Baby new potato with chargrilled pancetta and spring onion
Red and yellow cherry tomatoes with oak-aged balsamic and chive dressing
Chargrilled vegetables with pesto and Parmesan shavings
Tomato, buffalo mozzarella and avocado with pesto
Italian anti pasta
Chicory and walnut salad with soft-boiled egg dressing, chives and Parmesan crisps
Chicken caesar salad topped with bacon and focaccia croutons
Spinach and smoked duck salad with crumbled feta and crispy shallots

Puddings
Coconut tart with lemon zest and passion fruit mascarpone
Tart au citron served with fresh berries
Tropical fruit salad in lemongrass syrup with passion fruit ice-cream
Compote of autumn berries with thick cream
Sour cherry and black cherry cheesecake with mascarpone and an almond tuille
Pannacotta with mixed berries
Rhubarb pavlova with rhubarb tuille
Lime brûlée with almond crisp blackberries

Breakfast
If guests are arriving after dinner (from 10 pm) then it is usual and courteous to offer something hot after midnight. This is in any case a good idea, especially if alcohol is being served!

A hot dish such as kedgeree with coffee or tea and toast is a splendid idea and easy to prepare. It makes a good alternative to eggs (poached or scrambled) with or without the additional sausage, tomatoes and bacon.

Toast with something supplemented with masses of fresh fruit and fruit juices is another good idea; for the more informal, bacon (or vegetarian alternative) butties in the early hours are a treat!

Heated trays are a must. The oriental fire-resistant type heated with nightlights are good – they really do work. Mara Berni, owner of the London restaurant San Lorenzo, has been using a form of these for years to heat her secret-recipe crudité sauce. She and her husband, Lorenzo, use small earthenware pots heated by an internal nightlight. Anyone who has – like me on numerous occasions – burnt his or her tongue will confirm that these get *very* hot!

CAKE

There are many creative cake-makers around, so seek recommendations and find the one that you think will best meet your requirements. My favourite happens to be Val Oates whose company 'Let Them Eat Cake' has for many years made some incredible fantasies in cake both for my clients and for myself. Some have been almost too amazing to cut.

Most professional cake-makers need at least two or three weeks' notice to produce most cakes, and wedding cakes take a great deal longer. When I am caught short and find myself having to create an instant cake, I have found the easiest and most effective thing to do is to buy simple ready-made oblong angel cakes from a supermarket, join them together using honey or marzipan to form the required shape (for birthdays usually the shape of a number), and then totally cover the result with icing. I then finish with candles, the person's name written with ready-to-use coloured tubes of icing, and a big bow. If a more artistic effect is needed, ready-made coloured icing that you roll and cut into shape can be great fun and is not as difficult to use as you may think. If in doubt, practise with plasticine or similar first.

Natasha Cole with her brother and her cake at Annabel's on her 21st birthday.

DRINKS

No matter what you are celebrating, serving good cocktails or drinks will quickly get guests into the party mood. Whether you decide to serve champagne, wine, beer, mixes, a delicious fruit or wine cup, or cocktails, will depend on your personal taste and your budget. If help and budget are limited then mixes, fruit cups such as sangria and bowls of punch are a good idea because they are simple to prepare and guests can easily help themselves. Once you have made a bowl of punch or sangria you can easily add more of the same ingredients as the level drops and the party continues.

Bear in mind that the greater the number of guests the simpler the choice of drink should be. You might want to offer just red or white wine or a pre-mixed cocktail, but you should also offer water or soft drinks as an alternative. If you serve guests as they arrive from trays of ready-poured drinks, ensure that trays are not overloaded with glasses (twelve is ample) as it can be hazardous carrying too many around. And do not pour chilled drinks too far in advance otherwise they will be warm by the time the guests arrive. Then have the waiters (or your friends if you have not hired staff) circulating with bottles or jugs to top up the glasses.

The Bar

Everything connected to your event should be done with a view to making life easier for you and all those concerned, and a dispense bar is a practical asset in keeping all the necessary equipment for serving drinks at one station. A dispense bar with sufficient surfaces for sorting, serving, and stacking helps preserve order and keep things flowing smoothly. It is an especially efficient way of doing things if the drink is being served a distance from the kitchen.

To set up a dispense bar, you will need a selection of the following:

Refrigerator (if possible)
Suitable table (a trestle or collapsible picnic table is ideal)

Large tablecloth or sheets (to hide the front of the table/s)
Glasses
Jugs
Trays
Plastic bin or containers for storing bottles on ice
Ice buckets or bottle coolers
Ice
Corkscrew
Bottle opener
Bottle stoppers
Can opener
Measure
Drinking straws
Cocktail shaker – if serving mixes
Small sieve
Spoons
Knife
Drip trays
A bucket or supply of clean water for rinsing glasses (if necessary)
Bins or basins for collecting the discarded liquid remains from glasses
Bin liners and cleaning utensils (see box)
Rubber gloves or a pack of thin rubber hospital gloves
Teacloths or napkins
Rolls of paper towel
First-aid box
Sufficient light or candles
Nuts, olives, fresh mint, fruit, or whatever ingredients or garnishes you or the
    barman may require

KEEPING COOL

Blocks or large bags of ice can usually be ordered and delivered from your wine merchant, catering firm or local fishmonger or, in smaller quantities, from garages and supermarkets. Blocks of ice are especially helpful if you have to keep large amounts of drink or food fresh in a cold room. If you are providing champagne, the champagne house or retailer will normally supply sufficient ice buckets. To cool a large quantity of bottles, I have successfully used a baby's plastic bath filled with ice, and plastic bins are similarly very useful.

Containers

If you don't have a suitable punch bowl then large plastic basins or even a portable baby's bath work perfectly as alternatives. You can always disguise the appearance of the bath or basin by using pins or wire to attach vine leaves or a yard/metre or two of plastic cloth, both of which look very effective.

Jugs are useful for soft drinks and water. Glass is preferable but good plastic acceptable.

Glasses

Your local wine merchant should loan you sufficient glasses if you give him the drink order, otherwise you can arrange to hire them from a catering equipment supplier. Alternatively you may find it easier and just as economical to buy cheap glasses from shopping outlets or 'reject' shops, which usually have huge stocks of hotelware seconds.

When it comes to size it is more sensible to avoid small glasses (unless, of course, you are serving an after-dinner liqueur). They need constant refilling and so are a waste of time. Better to have large glasses or, for mixes filled with ice, long glasses. Apart from making the drink go further, most people are Americanised now and prefer ice with almost all their drinks.

PARTY DRINK AND COCKTAIL RECIPES

As my charming, very good friend Ian Wisniewski, the world's foremost authority on spirits and cocktails, says in his excellent, comprehensive book, *Party Cocktails*, 'Throughout the world, it is liquid refreshment that fuels our good times.' In his book (published by Conran Octopus), he details more than 170 recipes for every type of occasion – from all-time classics such as Martinis to non-alcoholic cocktails and even hangover cures – plus advice on serving and knocking them back!

Some time ago Ian conducted a series of master classes in making and appreciating cocktails. Although I enthusiastically attended each class, and at the end of the course received my certificate (giving me, I believe, a degree with honours in cocktail making and tasting!), my memory of the classes remains somewhat blurred... In fact I am sure that after the Martini class I completely lost a day, although I did discover 'straight up Margaritas' and 'dirty Martinis' were definitely my favourites! The following recipes are taken from Ian's book.

Margarita
    Wedge of lemon
    Salt, for rim of glass
    Ice cubes for shaker
    50 ml (1 tbsp) blanco (white or silver) tequila
    15 ml (1 tbsp) Cointreau (orange liqueur)
    25 ml (2½ tbsp.) lime juice

Wipe the lemon over the rim of a Martini glass to moisten it, then dip the rim into the salt.
    Into a shaker half-full with ice, pour the tequila, Cointreau and lime juice, and shake. Strain the cocktail into the glass, being careful not to dislodge the salt.

Dry Martini
    Ice cubes for mixing
    75 ml (5 tbsp.) gin or vodka
    10 ml (1½ tbsp.) dry vermouth
    Strip of lemon zest or a green olive for garnish

Place a few ice cubes in a mixing glass, add the gin or vodka and the dry vermouth, and stir. Strain into a Martini glass and garnish with the lemon zest or olive.

The front cover of The Red Cross London Ball programme.

Sangria
    (Makes about 5 litres/9 pints)
    Plenty of ice
    2 litres (3½ pints) sparkling lemonade
    3–4 750-ml-bottles red wine
    100 ml (4 fl oz) vodka (some may use gin although I do not)

Caster sugar, to taste
2 oranges, bananas and apples, peeled and sliced
1 cinnamon stick

Place plenty of ice in a large bowl. Pour in the lemonade, red wine, gin and vodka. Sprinkle in the sugar to taste, stir, then add the fruit and cinnamon and stir again. Taste and sprinkle in more sugar if required, stirring well to dissolve it before tasting again. Serve in tall glasses.

Hot glogg or punch
Ideally, this spiced and sweetened wine should be heated the day before (without the vodka) to allow the flavours to develop. When ready to serve, add the vodka and reheat gently.

(Serves 4–6)
1 bottle (750ml) red wine
2 cinnamon sticks
8 cloves
12 cardamom seeds
5 tsp caster sugar
150 ml (5½ fl oz) Absolut or other Swedish vodka
To serve: raisins and blanched almonds, with cinnamon sticks if desired

Drop a few raisins and blanched almonds into mugs or heatproof glasses. Set aside. Heat the wine and spices gently in a saucepan, stirring in the sugar until it dissolves, then add the vodka. Bring the liquid almost to the boil, then strain into the prepared mugs or glasses. Serve with cinnamon sticks, if desired.

WINES AND CHAMPAGNE

Good wine does not necessarily have to be expensive – there are some excellent inexpensive wines and champagnes around. Talk to a local wine merchant and, if possible, taste his suggestions and be guided by his expertise. Take time to do some research by contacting wine suppliers, or restaurants or hotels, and arrange to attend their tastings. Believe me, poor wine can be a disaster, especially in what it does for the heads of your guests the following morning.

Champagne takes its name from the region of northeastern France where it is made; a sparkling wine made anywhere else is termed sparkling wine (never champagne). When it comes to a special celebration you should try to stick to the real thing. If you really cannot stretch to champagne then take the greatest care to choose one of the better sparkling wines – there are some excellent ones. If there is no one to advise you properly, select one that has the words 'methode traditionelle'

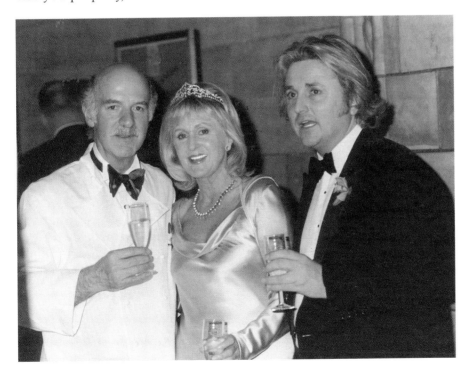

Anton Mosimann, Liz Brewer and David Emmanuel at Anton's 50th.

or 'methode champenoise' somewhere on the label as this indicates that the wine has been made using traditional champagne-making methods.

I have occasionally used Cava, especially when my client's budget has been limited, and I have served it ice cold with fresh peach juice or juice made from fresh raspberries or strawberries. Cava is in fact produced by 'methode champenoise'. It is a good alternative but it must be served ice cold.

Storing and Serving

Serving wine correctly is as important as choosing wine and, as my friend and mentor on party drinks, Ian Wisniewski, points out:

'The right serving temperature is crucial as this has an important influence on the way a wine tastes. White wines should be chilled to promote their character. Red wines should be served at room temperature and allowed some time to "breathe", either by decanting or by pouring a small amount into a glass to help the rest of the bottle "aerate". This helps the wine to reveal its full credentials. The appropriate style of glass should also be used, as this has an important influence on the way that aromas and flavours are conveyed: in order to breathe more easily a good red wine needs a larger breathing area so it requires the more open surface afforded by the larger rim; white wine is generally served in a smaller glass.'

Champagne

The quality of all champagne can be affected by the way it is both stored and poured. I am grateful to the Hon. Daniel Brennan, marketing manager of Laurent-Perrier UK, for the following advice:

'The addition of bubbles increases the need for good storage conditions and extra care when serving. Even the shape of a glass can have an effect on the intrinsic aromas and flavours of the champagne. Champagne should be stored, horizontally or vertically, at 12–18°C (53–64°F) out of direct light. It should be served at 4.5–7°C (40–45°F). When pouring champagne, pour a little into each glass first, then go back and top each one up to between two-thirds and three-quarters full. Pour it only when your guests are ready to drink: pre-poured champagne will lose its sparkle – the essence of champagne.'

SOFT DRINKS

More and more people these days limit their intake of alcohol – either for reasons of health or because they may be driving after the party. So have sufficient supplies of soft drinks available. It is a good idea to order more than required. In fact this applies to most drink as it can always be returned for refund or stored for later use.

Use jugs for soft drinks as they can then be mixed with ice. Jugs also enable you to add still or sparkling water, soda water or tonic, which will make the drink go further

WATER

Still or sparkling? The answer is that it is still best to offer both although frankly, if asked, I would reply that I am trying to rid my body of carbon dioxide so why would I want to increase levels by drinking sparkling water?

Bottled water is the most convenient. Filtered water is fine for small numbers of guests, but if you will have to do a great deal of filtering it is best to stick with bottled. Today – other than for very formal dining, when the wine waiter dispenses water – it is acceptable to place bottled water on the table alongside the wine.

If your celebration lasts many hours, there comes a time when guests have eaten and drunk sufficiently and require large quantities of filtered water. If your stocks of bottled water have run dry then jugs of filtered iced water with slices of lemon and cucumber will be very welcome.

'If music be the food
of love, play on'

William Shakespeare
Twelfth Night

branch 7

entertainment

MUSIC

Music, whether live or canned, can be a vitally important ingredient in the success of any event: it is most effective in helping to set the right mood and to create the desired atmosphere for the occasion. From the one-man band to the full-scale orchestra, and from light, background, taped music to the dance rhythms of disco, there is such tremendous scope when it comes to music that it really is worth giving your selection careful consideration.

Consider the programme of the party or event and decide when the various sounds or musical entertainment you have chosen will be most effective or appropriate. Work out a timetable pinpointing the stages at which one type of music or entertainment will be replaced by another. Bear in mind that gentle sounds such those of a harp are at their most effective during the early stages or quieter moments of an event, and will certainly be appreciated by guests that arrive promptly. As numbers

SOUND LEVELS

This is a matter of choice but, sensibly, the music needs to be loud enough to create atmosphere and to be appreciated but not so loud as to assault everyone's eardrums. There is nothing more annoying for guests when enjoying their meal, drink or conversation than having to strain to speak or to hear over the blast of a loud-speaker system. Neighbours that live within hearing distance must also be taken into consideration. As suggested in Branch 3, to avoid problems with neighbours it is sensible to let them know of the event in advance and, where possible, include them on the guest list.

increase and the chat gets louder, this kind of entertainment can be totally overpowered, so they need to either finish or if necessary, be replaced with something a little louder.

Background Music or Sound

Background music should produce enough sound to break the silence but not so much that it interferes with conversation. It is ideal for helping to avoid any awkward echoes in the atmosphere at the beginning of a special event or occasion, when the clock strikes the magical hour of arrival and the first guests begin to arrive. Other appropriate times for background music might be during the main meal, or even after dinner during the breaks in the band music or other entertainment.

Depending on the size and type of venue, live performers such as pianists, harpists, violinists, string quartets, wandering minstrels, or even a 'one-man-band', can be most effective in setting the tone and enhancing the ambience. You might like to choose sounds that are linked with your particular theme. It is relatively easy nowadays to obtain tapes of most background noises – the jungle, birds, bells, the sea, flowing water, and so on.

Discotheques and Bands

The choice of discotheque or band – indeed the decision to have live music or not – will be dictated by budget and personal preference. There are numerous mobile discotheques and bands to choose from so make certain that the one you select is reliable, comes highly recommended, and will provide the type of music you require at a fee that suits your budget.

If you have no choice but to select someone from the local directory or a local magazine be especially careful to obtain a number of reliable references and, if possible, arrange to watch the band or disc jockey performing at another event. Most bands will provide you with a demo tape or CD with a selection of their music that you can assess before you make a decision, but it is still preferable to see them performing live. In any case, it is extremely unwise to book a band – or even a disc jockey – without any idea of what they sound like and without making certain that their music selection suits your requirements.

The disc-jockey or band leader needs to arrive well in advance on the day to set up and to do sound and equipment checks. It is also very important to make certain your electricity output is sufficient for this equipment, especially if lighting is also provided.

The positioning of the disco and/or band will depend on your venue and the atmosphere you wish to achieve. If you are having a disco as well as a band, and space is limited, the disc jockey will need to position the decks and other paraphernalia so as not to interfere with the band's equipment. If you decide to have the disco set up in a separate area make certain it is safe and easy to access and exit.

CABARET

It is generally advisable to keep any cabaret performance to within an agreed time frame. When guests are in party mood their attention span is limited, so the golden rule is keep it short! However excellent and entertaining the cabaret may be, there will naturally come a point when guests want to chat or proceed to the next stage of the event. Don't risk letting them become bored or irritated. Nothing is worse for the performer or indeed for the atmosphere if a performer overplays his part and loses the attention of the audience.

Occasionally, getting the guests to join in – as is possible with magic shows, limbo dancing, and so on – can certainly warm up the atmosphere (although guests are unlikely to be keen participants if this kind of thing takes place too early in the evening). A surprise cabaret is always fun but, again, 'short and sharp' is the secret of success. A few years ago at a party in Paris, the surprise cabaret was Barry Humphries/Dame Edna Everidge. The host had cleverly fed him suitable anecdotes concerning some of the better-known guests. Dame Edna had a field day – much to everyone's amusement.

SPOTLIGHTS

Special performers and cabaret artists do benefit from spotlights. Well positioned they can make all the difference and enhance the performance. If the performer does not have his or her own spotlight, a good lighting technician can advise and supply.

Page 99: Ivana Trump and Henrik Jönsson attempting to do the Gay Gordon at Skibo Castle.

A singer who will perform whilst mingling with the audience can be highly entertaining – and particularly flattering for those being serenaded. Choosing a comedian needs more careful consideration. Nothing destroys an atmosphere quicker than flat jokes!

OTHER PERFORMERS

Performers welcoming guests quickly puts people in the party mood. If you are not leaving the suggestions and selection to a party organizer, caterer, or band, you might consider using one of the many highly talented students or buskers that perform day and night in prime public locations (usually in city squares) throughout the country. Most notable of the London locations are Leicester Square and Covent Garden, where performers welcome the opportunity of contributing to a special occasion for a very reasonable fee. Circus performers, conjurers, balloon sculptors – there are many colourful acts to choose from to add flavour to your event.

Trumpeters of the Household Division also make a magnificent and definite statement, especially before an important announcement or entrance. A formal approach should be made to the Brigade Major of the Household Division, Horse Guards, Whitehall, London SW1.

CONTROL AND SOUND SYSTEMS

When installing control and sound systems, it is essential to check that the power supply is sufficient to cope with the load placed upon it. It is also important to ensure that the sound boxes are directed towards the area or areas where you wish the sound to be focused, leaving other, quieter areas that are more conducive to making conversation.

The most important thing if you are setting up your own systems is to make certain you know what you are doing; otherwise, get proper expert advice and *don't take risks*. You don't want to electrocute your guests (or yourself), or blow the system and end up with no power. This very nearly happened to me years ago during one of the first charity events I organized. It was pouring with rain, and my electrician suddenly discovered that the power box had lost its cover and was half filled with water. Another inch and it is more than likely that the 300 guests and I would have been cinders!

DANCING

Wherever dancing is planned as part of the entertainment, discourage people from taking glasses or cigarettes on to the dance floor. Broken glass and cigarette burns are the most frequent cause of injury, accident or plain annoyance. If you have no one available to keep an eye on this then make certain the disc jockey or band leader takes on this responsibility. In the event of a glass getting broken it is advisable to have given instructions to stop the music, clear the floor and either summon help to clean the spillage or have utensils handy for one of the performers to do this.

Scottish Reels and Other Group Dancing

To get everyone warmed up and circulating it can be a good idea to have a few simple Scottish reels, some country barn dancing, or even variations of the American type of line dancing. Scottish reels were originally designed for precisely this purpose: to give everyone a chance to meet or at least to dance with fellow guests. Many of the early English dances were also designed to encourage guests to dance with a variety of partners.

If you do not know how to do the various group dances then either hire a couple of professionals who will lead the guests through the steps and quickly get them to join in or take a few lessons yourself, encouraging guests to do likewise. You could even suggest suitable classes so they can have a few rehearsals before the event. This can be a great deal of fun, and information on classes can usually be found in most local papers or magazines.

PERFORMERS' REQUIREMENTS

Most performers require a small changing room, WC facilities and refreshments. If you do not have a suitable room then a small tent could work as an alternative as could a screened-off area supplied with a mirror, small table, chair, a hook or hangers for coats and, where necessary, costume.

For some inexplicable reason the rumba continues to thrive – even at the more conservative dances. To take part you need to be feeling very stupid or very drunk!

Dance Card

The old-fashioned dance card – still used at hunt balls and grand balls in Scotland – is a quaint and fun way to get people moving around meeting each other early in the evening.

Ensuring that everyone receives and uses the dance cards does take a little organizing but the general rule is to give one to each guest on arrival. Attached to the card should be a small pencil for listing and numbering each reel and/or dance. The guests must then choose different partners for all the named dances. Once a proposed dance partner has agreed, the guest must write the partner's name on the appropriate line on the card.

Guests should make certain they nab their partners as quickly as possible in order to get their cards filled. It is then the duty of both parties to find their relevant partners before each dance.

The dance card.

PARTY GAMES

Party games can be tremendous fun and are quite often enormously entertaining. They are also a good way of encouraging guests to really communicate and bond. Charades is a typical example: the suggestion to play is invariably greeted with quite a few groans, but once the game gets going it is great fun, very competitive, and often memorable. I'll never forget one such occasion, which occurred at a weekend house party at Ayton Castle, on the borders of Scotland. Charades was suggested by my host, David Liddle-Grainger, following a delightful, black-tie dinner for thirty guests. One particular woman, known for her formidable character and reserved attitude, totally floored the entire gathering with her astounding, frank, and very memorable interpretation of 'Fanny by Gaslight'!

Charades

For this game you will need paper, pencils or pens, and a bowl, hat or other container.

Divide guests into two teams. The easiest way to do this is to pick two team leaders who take turns to choose the members of their team from amongst the guests. Decide on which subjects will be the topic of the charades. Usual categories are books, films, TV shows and theatre. One team goes into another room so both teams have privacy. Each member of the team has to think of an original title within the chosen categories, which is then written on a piece of paper, folded and put in a hat or bowl. It is a good idea to have a time limit for this of say ten minutes, after which everyone returns to the main room.

One member of one team starts. He is either given or takes at random one of the folded slips of paper from the opposite team. He reads the title on the paper and then quickly decides how to mime it to his team so that they will be able to guess what it is as quickly as possible. The player is allowed a set time to do this. To make it easier for the team to interpret the player's silent gesturing, the player will usually mime one word at a time. There are some standard gestures to indicate the following:

Liz with couturier Eric Way trying to mime *My Fair Lady* at Shakespeare's Globe.

A book – by opening both hands outwards as if opening a book.

A film – by using the hands to mime the action of an imaginary clapper board.

A play – by using the hands to mime the drawing back of stage curtains.

A TV programme – by drawing a square in the air with the fingers.

The number of words in the title – by holding up the necessary number of fingers.

The first word in the title – by holding up one finger; the second word can be indicated by holding up two fingers, the third by three, and so on.

This word 'sounds like' – by pulling the ear and then miming a word that rhymes with the one in the title.

A small word such as 'a', 'and', 'the' and so on – by closing the forefinger and thumb together.

The whole title – by using both hands to describe a circle in the air.

If necessary, long words can be broken up into syllables; if one word is particularly difficult to mime the player can move on to the next, hoping that the team will not need it in order to guess the full title. Whatever happens the player must continue to be silent. He can indicate when someone gets a word right or wrong by nodding or shaking his head.

So, for example, if you are miming *A Town Like Alice* you would open both hands to indicate a book, and then mime the clapper board to indicate that it has also been made into a film. You would then show four fingers indicating a title of four words and then one finger to show that you are going to describe the first word, which would be done by closing the finger and thumb to indicate tiny word. When the team guesses the first word you move on to the second, which could be mimed by pulling your ear (sounds like) and frowning, from which you hope you team might get 'town'. You continue in this way until the team shouts out the correct title.

Sardines

This game needs a large house and perhaps a garden. It can be great fun and somewhat intimate – as I discovered when I once chose the largest bed in the house in which to flatten myself and hide. I was in Ireland at the time with a boyfriend called Bill. Our relationship was never quite the same after the sardine episode!

One guest is given five minutes to go off and hide. The hiding place must be large enough to accommodate most of the others playing the game either in the same space or near by. The remaining guests follow one by one, seeking out the hiding place. If they find the person hiding they join him or her and remain quiet until all but one of the players have also found the place. The last person to arrive is the loser. The winners are the rest who, by the end of the game, are naturally very close friends!

Murder in the Dark

This can be played in several different ways. This version was invented by my good friend Anton Kristensen to spice up his infamous house

An ideal hiding place for sardines.

parties at his cottage on Earl Spencer's estate at Althorp. Take identical pieces of paper, one for each guest, and write the word 'Murderer' on one of them. All the pieces should then be folded up, placed in a hat or bowl and shuffled before asking each guest to take one piece of paper from the hat and to look at it without allowing anyone else to see it. At this point, only the person who draws the piece of paper bearing the word murderer will know who the murderer is (or will be).

Turn off the lights and close the doors to contain the game in a limited space. Then all the guests, including the murderer, stumble around the room bumping into each other. When the murderer is finally ready to commit murder he may do so in whatever way has been stipulated before play commenced. Usual and most intriguing is for the murderer to kiss or hug his victim. The victim must then scream and lie down. The murderer will then quickly move away from the victim and look innocent before the lights are turned on again. The object of the game is then for everyone, including the victim, to guess who the murderer is. In doing this each person is allowed to ask three questions. Some people are recognizable by certain features, such as height, length of hair, and so on. So the art of the game is in the murderer's ability to fool everyone: if he is tall he might move round the room with legs bent; if slim he might add a pillow to his middle and so on. A silly game but fun.

The Hat Game

This game, taught to me by my friends David and Elizabeth Coaten, is a bit like musical chairs but not quite so rowdy! Ask each guest to bring a hat or make certain you can supply one for all but one of your guests. The more bizarre the hats the better. Guests stand front to back in a circle and, as music plays, they pass their hats backwards to the person behind. When the music stops, they must place whatever hat they happen to have on their heads. Since they will have started one hat short there will be one person who is hatless when the music stops. This person is 'out'. Each time this happens another hat is taken out of play so that there is always one hat short. The winner is the last person wearing a hat.

Liz Brewer with a 'waiter' at Simon Drake's House of Magic.

FIREWORKS

Fireworks are great fun and now very sophisticated. They can make a brilliant end to an evening or provide an exciting interlude during a special celebration; even a short blast of well-selected fireworks is exhilarating. However, unless you really know what you are doing – or you have help from someone who does – firework displays are best left to the professionals. A great success on a number of birthday parties has been to have the person's name illuminated in fireworks at the end of a dramatic short display. The effect is worth the expense but it does need to be created professionally.

Opposite page:
Top left: A 'Living Phallus' at Ash and Gita Tandon's party.
Top right: The 'Up and Down Soldiers' at Claridges.
Bottom left: Ivana Trump, Cameron Mackintosh and Shirley Bassey at the One Aldwych party.
Photograph by Xpressions Photography
Bottom right: A 'Balloon Man' at Anton Mosimann's 50th birthday party at the Natural History Museum.

'*Unfortunately, some people don't hear you until you scream*'

Stefanie Powers

branch 8

staff and helpers

Adequate and efficient help is a most important factor, especially if you, as well as the guests, want to enjoy the occasion. If you do not know the people you are hiring then make certain you thoroughly check their references. When you are using an approved catering firm then it is their job to make certain their staff are up to scratch, but find out whatever you can before the event as there is not much point in protesting afterwards (other than perhaps to gain a refund) as you and most probably your guests will have had a rotten time.

If your budget doesn't run to hired help then recruit a few close friends, or their kids. In my experience kids love to help, especially if you give them a little incentive! And friends also enjoy helping, especially those who find parties daunting as it gives them a good reason to circulate in a natural way while at the same time being a great help to you. If disaster strikes and you suddenly find yourself stuck with no help then honesty is the best policy. Explain your predicament to early arrivals who will, with any luck, offer to muck in. My 'just in case' tip

Ian Watson and two helpers.

is always to have a few fun aprons or even French maids outfits with which to deck out game guests (this can give a whole new slant to your party!)

DOORMEN

When entertaining more than a few close friends it is advisable to have help with opening the door so that you are free to look after the guests, make introductions and circulate.

Car jockeys are also very useful, especially in cases where the car park is more than a short distance away from the venue. They will take the car from the driver on arrival, give him or her a ticket, and take care of the parking efficiently and safely. When the guest is ready to depart, the car jockey will, on presentation of the ticket, fetch and return the car.

GREETERS

On occasions when there are a number of hosts, it is usual for them to line up at the entrance in order to greet the guests as they arrive. If for some reason the host is not familiar with all the guests then either an MC (master of ceremonies – *see* opposite) or an official greeter can receive each guest on arrival, take the person's name, and announce him or her to the host/s.

BUTLERS

The main duties of a butler are to answer the door, announce the arrival of guests, and serve drinks. Nowadays the butler's duties are less clearly defined than they used to be and often extend to preparing the glasses, the drinks, the ice, and on occasions the canapés. Butlers normally wear either black tie or a dark suit. White gloves are sensible and a good idea for the obvious reason that they are reassuring of cleanliness.

MASTER OF CEREMONIES & TOASTMASTERS

A competent MC is a bonus to any special event – an asset not only in aiding the co-ordination of the occasion, but also in the following:

- Directing and announcing the guests.
- Prompting the host and ensuring the correct order of events.
- Saying Grace.
- Proposing an appropriate toast.
- Introducing speakers and performers, and making other announcements, such as the Loyal Toast, and the all too frequent request to remove a badly parked car.

I'll never forget attending a private birthday party at London Zoo when the MC announced, 'Would the owner of car registration number XXXXX kindly move it now or the elephants will!'

Yes, unfortunately, it was mine!

There are schools that teach the art of being an accomplished MC and/or butler, and these are a good place to start when seeking a suitable MC, as is The Royal Guild of Toastmasters. There are also well-known MCs who add extra sparkle. One of the best known of these is Ivor Spencer, who is the first toastmaster to have officiated at over 1,000 royal events and who is also famous for his International School for Butlers and Professional Toastmasters.

COOK OR CHEF

Today, with the numerous television programmes dominated by celebrity chefs teaching us all how simple it is to create those tempting culinary wonders, it is hard to believe that there are still people, like myself, who are complete idiots in the kitchen. To my shame, the first time I attempted to cook after returning from honeymoon, the fire engines arrived having been alerted by the neighbours who had seen smoke billowing out of the rear windows. At the time I was happily

PHOTOGRAPHY AND/OR VIDEO

It is worth having this done professionally by one of the numerous specialists in the field. However, if the budget does not stretch then either get an enthusiastic and reliable friend to help out, or do it yourself (remembering to have ample supplies of film, the necessary batteries, *and* a spare camera!) Alternatively, a novel idea is to distribute throw-away cameras amongst the guests with instructions for them to take as many photographs as possible and return the finished cameras to you before they depart.

Opposite page: Two helpers.

wallowing in my bath having completely forgotten the rather nasty frozen spinach I was attempting to defrost without water in a saucepan. I haven't improved, which is why at home I eat raw!

If you are using the full services of a professional catering company, you will not have to worry about engaging a chef or cook as this will be done by the firm. If, however, you are doing the catering yourself, but need a chef or other staff to help in the kitchen, you will have to make your own arrangements. If you do not know anyone who can recommend a chef, you can contact a catering firm or agency who will supply staff only, or you can approach a good catering school who may be able to recommend one of the students. In any case, it is wise to get references – you cannot afford to wait until the chef is in the kitchen to discover that the only thing he or she can create is havoc.

WAITING STAFF

Waiters and waitresses can be hired through agencies or through the caterers, or you may find them through friends' recommendation. Even your local restaurant may help out if you give them some warning. Waiters normally charge by the hour, plus an amount for travel if they have to work late. If you are doing the recruiting bear in mind that waiters and waitresses do not automatically come dressed in uniform, so ask what they normally wear and make certain they understand your dress preference if you have one. (If you wish to impose a particular uniform you may have to supply it or cover the cost of hiring it.) It is also a good idea to check the applicant's nails. Dirty nails are unhygienic and give a bad impression to the guests.

CLOAKROOM & LAVATORY ATTENDANTS

Anything over twenty coats can cause havoc when guests are leaving, and it can spoil things enormously if someone has difficulty finding his or her coat. There is also the risk that a coat may go home on the wrong

Robert Hay and his helpers.

back – a frequent occurrence at the end of a good party. It looks the same, may feel the same, but the following morning the horrifying realization – you took the wrong coat! It's even worse when house or car keys are in the pocket. If you decide not to arrange for professional cloakroom attendants then see if you can persuade your kids or a friend to help keep order.

CLEANERS

Having to clear up after a particularly wonderful, wild, and memorable celebration can really throw a damper on the whole joy of hosting, so this is definitely an area where it is well worth having help. Once again, the catering firm or agency should be able to provide or recommend suitable staff.

Every year I co-host a professionally catered picnic party at Royal Ascot for an average of a hundred guests. Oh the joy of walking away at the end of lunch to watch the first race, knowing that when I return to my car all will be spotless without even a trace of a champagne cork on the ground! So make certain that you get sufficient hands to clean up as soon as possible after the last guest departs.

Fairy elf helpers.
Photograph: Edward Lloyd

'Welcome the coming, speed the parting, guest'

Alexander Pope

Odyssey, Book 1

branch 9

the morning after

At the end of a really good party, there is always a huge trail of debris of a quantity that never ceases to amaze me – though it should be said that it is usually a sign that a very good time has been had by all.

If you have decided not to get professional help for the clearing up then invite some game friends to a 'clearing-up' brunch, lunch or supper. There are bound to be edible (and liquid) leftovers to feed you all and, let's face it, you might just as well enjoy yourself whilst doing dreary, 'after the event' chores.

It helps enormously if you have kept everything clean and orderly during the initial setting-up process and (wherever possible) during the event. A vacuum cleaner, dustpan and brush, brooms, mops, dusters, and of course bin liners, are the essentials to have on hand at all times. In my experience you can never have enough bin-liners. Bin liners can be used not just to collect the mess, but for gathering tablecloths and napkins ready for the wash, and for storing the remains of the decor so that it is ready to be used on another suitable occasion or returned.

Previous page: Lighting expert John Bloomfield – who has been one of my greatest helpers over the past twenty-five years – the morning after the Magical Fashion Fantasia.

RETURNABLES

The important thing to remember about returnables is to return them as soon as possible – preferably undamaged and as you received them. If you don't do this immediately you may forget and incur a penalty payment for late return. If you have paid a deposit make certain it is returned or deducted from the final account.

DAMAGE AND BREAKAGE

Damage does happen. If an item is damaged or broken while in your care, check your insurance to see whether you are covered, and inform the supplier as soon as possible as it may take time to replace. This is not only courteous but also correct procedure. There is normally a charge for any breakage, but whether or not this is imposed will depend on your relationship with the supplier.

PHOTOGRAPHS

The important thing about photographs is to get the films developed immediately after the event and put them into a special album. It is often the case that if you don't do this promptly it doesn't get done. Having the photographs and any other items such as a copy of the invitation, menu, guest list, and so on, arranged in an album will give you and your friends a great deal of pleasure. If you have the time and patience, sort photos and send them to the various guests as this is always greatly appreciated.

LOST PROPERTY

Unfortunately there is always someone who loses an item or leaves it behind. This might be an item of clothing, a mobile phone, a camera or a valuable piece of jewellery (usually an earring). Make certain all items found during the clearing up process are listed and stored safely in the hope that the owner will discover the loss and make contact. If the item is valuable it is best to inform the local police as soon as possible: it sometimes happens that the owner does not miss the item for a few days and then, on discovering that it is missing, does not immediately remember when it was last seen or worn. For insurance purposes the owner will have to inform the police who, it is hoped, will have a record of it from you.

Preparation is everything, even when clearing up! Liz and a helper.

'One might well say that man is divisible into two great classes: hosts and guests'

Max Beerbohm
And Even Now: Hosts and Guests

celestial sun and moon

DUTIES OF THE HOST

Looking after the Guests

The most important duty of any host is to look after his or her guests. This may seem obvious, but too often it is a duty that is not properly respected and observed. It is simply not good enough to greet and move guests on by saying something like, 'Great to see you – enjoy yourself,' or 'Hello – have a drink I'll catch up with you later.'

Guests should never be left stranded and having to fend for themselves. If you don't have a huge amount of confidence there is nothing worse than suddenly arriving in a room full of people you have never seen before. Even if you are capable of plucking up enough courage to introduce yourself to a nearby group of fellow guests, you may find yourself feeling even more awkward: the English still regard the unsolicited approach as an inavasion of their space and may be less than truly welcoming or, worse, condescending.

Ivana Trump and 'Living Statue' at the Magical Fashion Fantasia for National Kidney Research Fund held at the Millenium Hotel, London.

It is the duty of a host to make his guests feel comfortable. If a mistake is made the host should either soothe ruffled feathers in the most diplomatic way possible or make less of the mishap with a light-hearted joke. I remember helping with a charity dinner in Istanbul to benefit what is now the Worldwide Fund for Wildlife. The guest of honour was His Royal Highness The Duke of Edinburgh. The service during dinner was a little slow, so a couple of guests at the top table, where I was sitting, started to stack the plates. There was a look of grave concern on several faces – after all, was this not a dreadful faux pas in front of the guest of honour? His Royal Highness noticed the concern, as did my charming hosts, Saeed and Sema Rabb Cerrahoglu, who both immediately started to help stack the plates and pass them to a waiter – with help from His Royal Highness, who remarked, 'Why not? We often do this back home!'

Circulating and Introducing Guests

The success of most gatherings is in the ability of the host to keep guests circulating. A good host will go from group to group, adding a new sparkle to the conversation and introducing people where necessary. The Duke of Bedford would – whenever possible – personally serve drinks to his guests. In this way, he was able to circulate and talk to each guest but have a good excuse to move on: in order to serve more drinks and greet new guests.

If a guest is standing alone the host should either personally in-troduce him or her to fellow guests or, if occupied or unable to perform this duty until later in the evening, make certain a colleague or co-host is capable of doing this. At any gathering people need help to circulate and be introduced. Nowadays, it is quite normal to have a person specifically employed to act in this capacity, moving people around and making certain guests are looked after and happy.

As a general rule, the host should introduce a younger person to an elder, a man to a woman, a junior rank to a senior, and so on. For example, 'Mrs Suitable Guest, this is John Other Guest,' or 'Jane Elder, may I introduce Janet Younger.' When introducing someone to a titled guest, it is usually safest to use formal social address unless you know the titled person prefers to be introduced otherwise. (*See* Appendix 2, Forms of Address.) It is important to speak clearly to ensure that both parties hear the other's name – it is embarrassing to have to ask someone's name when you have only just been introduced. (Having said this, if the host has forgotten one or both names, speaking indistinctly is one cheeky way of overcoming the problem!)

Making Conversation

As the host you have the advantage of knowing your guests (or at least most of them) and are therefore able to blend them together with appropriate conversation starters, such as, 'John, you design tables don't you? – well, Niki here just loves dancing on them.' Having said your bit to break the ice, swiftly move on. If you can say something witty or amusing, all the better as it will give them something to laugh or chat about.

The art of good conversation is in knowing how to listen rather than talk, so learn to make others talk and take a genuine interest in what they have to say. The more you listen, the more you will find that questions spring to mind to prevent the conversation from drying up. If you find yourself out of your depth do not be afraid of asking for more explanation: more often than not the person speaking will be flattered by your interest. Do not play too helpless, however, for even if you are a woman (and therefore perhaps more likely to get away with it) this can be irritating.

Dealing with Difficult Situations

Drunken guests

A drunken guest needs to be gently but firmly removed with as much discretion as possible. Either put the person in a spare bedroom or call a cab to take the person home. Do this quickly and with a degree of authority to avoid any arguments.

TOASTS

A toast is the call to drink in honour of a person or occasion. Traditionally, smoking is not permitted until after the toasts. The Loyal Toast, in honour of the Sovereign, is normally done after the main course. The Loyal Toast, which is done by the host, MC, butler or head waiter, is simply 'The Queen,' or 'Ladies and Gentlemen, the Queen.' (If titled guests are present this would be preceded by the title of whoever was present, e.g. 'My Lords Ladies and Gentleman, The Queen.' The guests repeat the name of the person being toasted and then take a sip of wine, port, or whatever they are drinking (but never water, which is considered unlucky).

Awkward guests

Be diplomatic but firm. If it looks as though someone is out to make trouble and ruin a good atmosphere, guide the person away and introduce him or her to another group of people in the hope that the incident will be forgotten. Another ploy is to apologise to each party and join them, deliberately changing the subject to diffuse the situation. If the guest persists in being rude or difficult and is determined to make trouble, then ask them to leave.

Gatecrashers

This is never an easy situation. Sometimes it happens innocently, such as when an invited guest turns up with an unexpected escort. However, if you do not know the person or can see no explanation for their presence, take them quietly to one side and ask whether they have an invitation. From their response you should be able to assess whether this is or is not a real mistake. Do not be embarrassed. If there has been a genuine mistake or oversight, no harm will have been done by your enquiries, but if the person is quite obviously a gatecrasher you have every right to be firm and politely ask them to leave, explaining that it is a private celebration. If they resist, which does happen – as in my experience gatecrashers are incredibly thick-skinned and take great offence at being found out and evicted – get help from a suitable strong-armed guest or, in an extreme case, call the police.

Some people are known to go to unbelievable lengths to gatecrash a good party, and the various tricks they use are often very simple but effective. One particular woman, well known for gatecrashing large prestigious events, telephones the organizer or the RSVP contact seen on a friend's invitation and merely accepts, adding a title to her name. She then explains that she has unfortunately mislaid the invitation and asks for a replacement, giving her private address. This ploy still appears to work for her.

Most gatecrashers are undesirables, and are more often than not a bunch of freeloaders who contribute very little to a well-planned occasion. They are definitely not an added attraction – if they were worth inviting they probably wouldn't need to resort to gatecrashing.

Hostess Gifts

A charming gesture originally made popular in America and continental Europe is to arrange gifts for the guests. This is especially welcoming to guests if they have travelled a long distance and are staying at an hotel, house party, or other accommodation.

As the general trend in recent years is for a major celebration such as a wedding to extend over two or three days, the gift might be left with an itinerary of the planned activities as well as a greeting from the host or hostess. This shows a great deal of thought and will be especially appreciated by the guests who have travelled overseas. An excellent example of how beautifully this can be done was the occasion of Elizabeth Collet's marriage to Dr Steven Funk, which took place in the wine country in the area around the Napa Valley, California. Upon the guests' arrival at their hotel on Thursday evening they found a 'Welcome Basket' in their rooms. It was a tin bucket (for that authentic 'country' feel) filled with gifts that had been carefully selected for their relevance to the region or for their significance to the bride or groom. They included a bottle of fine Napa Valley wine, a silver corkscrew engraved with the bride's and bridegroom's initials and the wedding date, a hand-tied bag of local candied walnuts, a wedge of locally made blue cheese and raisin-and-nut crackers, some lemon ginger biscotti (homemade by a friend), and a pouch of five candy-covered almonds (with a card explaining the local tradition of having almonds at weddings). The attached, handwritten envelope contained a welcome letter as well as a list of the various weekend events and a local map bearing stickers indicating the location of each event.

On Friday night, when the guests came home from the rehearsal dinner, they found a bottle of olive oil (made at the estate where the wedding would be held the next day) accompanied by a card explaining the special significance of the olive oil and wishing the guests a

The gifts presented to every guest at the wedding of Dr Steven Funk and Elizabeth Collet in Napa Valley, USA.
Photograph: Michelle Pattee

wonderful night's sleep. This was followed on Saturday night by a gift of handmade chocolate truffles presented in a handmade box bearing a gorgeous sugar dragonfly.

The gifts described here make for an exceptional example of the degree of creativity and thought that can be given to the preparation of gifts for guests. However, hostess gifts do not have to be extravagant, nor do they have to be so numerous in order to be worth having. They can be a simple flower, chocolates, or a selection of small appropriate items. They can be left in the bedroom of each guest to greet them on their arrival, or they can be placed on the dining table (*see* Branch 5). Whatever they are, gifts from the hostess are always appreciated by guests and can help to make an occasion feel extra special.

DUTIES OF THE GUEST

Replying to Invitations

The golden rule is answer promptly! It is rude and inconsiderate to leave your reply to the last minute, and it is unforgivable not to reply at all. This is especially important if you cannot attend: the sooner you decline an invitation the more time it gives the host to fill the gap. Culprits are usually those people who do not themselves entertain and are therefore unaware of how difficult it is to arrange something when the final numbers are unknown. There have been times in the past when I have been arranging a large seated dinner for 200 or so guests and have sent out 150 invitations – some to singles and some to doubles. One week before the event, only 50 per cent of the invitees have replied. I have then had to try to decide whether I should cater for 75 guests or for 300 (as might happen if all the invitees come and all the singles bring a date!). As you can see this makes the host's or organizer's life extremely difficult. I now have the names of those guests who do not reply removed from the main list kept at door control. This usually ensures that if they are ever invited again they will remember to answer.

If you have been invited as a single person and wish to bring a friend you must call your host and ask if this is possible. It is inconsiderate and bad manners simply to turn up with an unexpected guest, and it can also be embarrassing (for all parties) if the numbers are restricted. In addition, it is worth remembering that you cannot always assume that your guest is unknown to the host; it might even be that the proposed person is not the flavour of the month and has been deliberately excluded from the original guest list!

While unexpected guests of singles can cause inconvenience, do not assume that the same does not apply if you have been invited as a couple and one of you does not attend: always let your host know your intentions.

Presents for the Host or Hostess

Give some thought in advance to presents. It really is not the cost of the gift that matters, but the thought and trouble it shows you have taken. Even those people who you presume must have everything will be touched by a small handmade or original gift.

Presentation is important too. The way you wrap and tie a present adds to the glamour of a gift. Make certain to include a small card so the recipient will know who gave the gift. If the card is attached to the outside, make sure it is properly secure: so often these cards fall off, leaving the host with the embarrassing challenge of trying to work out who gave what.

Giving wine to your host at a dinner or cocktail party is not always a good idea unless it is a good wine or champagne. If you do bring a bottle, don't expect your wine to be served unless you are attending a 'bottle party'. A good host will normally have preselected and prepared the appropriate wines for the occasion.

Timing

Unless indicated otherwise, it is generally acceptable to arrive approximately ten to thirty minutes after the stated time although the

so – without feeling uncomfortable – is to say how much you hope they have enjoyed themselves and how much you have enjoyed entertaining them and hope to see them again very soon. This should be done in a light way and with good humour. If necessary you may at the same time gently guide them towards the door or to wherever they need to collect their coats. The vast majority will immediately get the message. Alternatively, half an hour or so after the time indicated, stop the drink being served and instruct the waiters or helpers to start politely collecting the glasses while you pleasantly and quietly explain that the party is over. Try to do this without putting too much of a damper on the atmosphere.

precise degree of leeway depends on the type of occasion. It is incorrect and inconsiderate to arrive before the appointed time. On the other hand to arrive very late is rude, especially if the occasion is seated – so you had better have a really good excuse!

Whether arriving late or leaving early the guest should do so discretely with the minimal amount of fuss so as not to spoil the atmosphere and break up the party. If you know in advance that you will be doing either, it is best to let the host know.

Knowing when to leave

The golden rule is don't overstay your welcome!

Deciding when to leave a party is not difficult if the intended departure time was indicated on the invitation. One of the main reasons for indicating a departure time is so that the host can warn the waiters, or general help and staff, how long they will be needed, so it is important that guests try to adhere to it. A pre-determined departure time is also helpful for guests who need to arrange cars or cabs or forewarn the babysitter.

If no departure time is indicated, you will need to use some common sense. The host will not normally indicate to you that it is time to go, so be considerate. Be aware of the passing of time and, if you think it is getting late, mention that you ought to be leaving, even if everything is still going full steam. It is then up to the host to protest and persuade you to stay.

When you do take your leave, it is not necessary to go around the room bidding everyone goodbye. A general farewell is sufficient plus a personal thank you and goodbye to your host or hostess.

Thanking the Host

It is kind and polite to your host to show your appreciation for all his or her effort by saying thank you after the event. Of course, you will have thanked the host on the point of departure, but this does not absolve you from the duty of sending a thank you afterwards. Put yourself in the host's place the following day or days after, wondering whether your guests enjoyed themselves. Flowers, a phone call, a card, an email or even a fax are in order. A handwritten letter is charming but in today's busy world the other alternatives are acceptable and appreciated.

If you really did not have a good time and therefore think it would be hypocritical to thank your host then do not (although you may not be invited again!). Whatever you choose to do, don't waste time: do it as soon as possible. If you mean what you write or say it will not be difficult. Try to let the host know how much you enjoyed yourself (this is especially convincing and charming if you can say why). But don't invent words: sincerity is important.

If you came as a guest of an invitee, do not leave it up to the invitee to thank the host on your behalf. It is courteous to send your own thank you; in any case this will give the host the means to contact you should they wish to invite you again.

The Kornfeld wedding.

DRESS CODES

Deciding what to wear to a formal event or gathering can be a minefield for guests, especially for women for whom the various dress codes can be interpreted in various ways. (It is notable that the terms used to describe a style of dress refer to men's attire, not women's.) So, for men it is a lot simpler: the codes are prescriptive, so unless a man is keen to demonstrate a little individual flair he need not give the matter much thought. All formal dress for men demands jacket, trousers, shirt and tie (and sometimes shoes and hat) of particular types, with accessories to include a clean white handkerchief in the breast pocket, and cufflinks.

'Black Tie'
For men Black Tie indicates single or double-breasted dinner suit (referred to in the United States as a tuxedo); the single-breasted

For those of Scottish descent with family tartan, highland dress is no problem. For others, Black Tie is acceptable at formal balls in the highlands and lowlands, but the best plan is to hire the correct attire. (Good hosts will often recommend outfitters.) Alternatives to the kilt are tartan trews, or silk breaches with silken hose. Women wear long evening gowns, with (if entitled to it) a tartan sash usually worn from the shoulder to the waist, depending on the status of the woman. For example, the daughter of a clan chief would wear it in one way while a wife will wear her husband's tartan in another. Evening shoes suitable for performing highland reels are vital. Don't make the mistake I made not so long ago: owing to lack of time I carelessly packed elegant but ridiculous 6-inch heels, and a slim gown with train, to attend the Angus Ball at Blair Castle. You can imagine the difficulty I had with anything more strenuous than the Dashing White Sergeant!

suit should preferably be worn with a waistcoat A stylish jacket, such as a Nero jacket or velvet smoking jacket (worn normally at an 'at home' in winter) is acceptable. A white jacket is for warm summer evenings and hot climates only. The appropriate shirt is a dress shirt (with turn-down, not winged, collar), silk polo neck or, nowadays, a smart black T-shirt. The tie is a bow tie, floppy bow tie, or even a diamond pendant. Shoes are black patent leather, velvet, or monogrammed evening pumps (which are generally worn for an 'at home'). Cummerbunds should *never* be worn except with single-breasted white tuxedo or when absolutely necessary to cover a large girth!

Today, women's Black Tie attire includes various types of dress from long evening gown to short frock. Tiaras should be reserved for White Tie occasions.

'White Tie' or 'Evening Dress'

This indicates a very formal, grand occasion so the dress code is more rigid than it is for Black Tie.

For men White Tie means black tails, starched white shirt (with stiff stand-up or winged collar), white bow tie, white waistcoat, both with studs, and black patent evening shoes. Morning coat is incorrect. The invitation will indicate whether decorations should be worn. On White Tie occasions, Black Tie is acceptable if necessary but it will make the wearer stand out, so it is worth making the effort to hire or borrow.

For women White Tie means long evening gowns. Trousers, however well designed for the evening, should never be worn. Long gloves (to be worn with sleeveless gowns) and tiaras are no longer de rigeur but they do tend to flatter and enhance the total look. (Although it is no longer a rule, tiaras are traditionally worn only by married women.)

Hunt Balls

Men should wear red tailcoat if they are a member of a hunt; otherwise Black Tie or White Tie as stipulated. Red tailcoat is worn with starched white shirt, white bow tie, white waistcoat (both with studs) and black patent evening shoes. Don't make the mistake of borrowing or wearing a red tailcoat without knowing which hunt it signifies. Be aware that each hunt has its own special buttons, and the collar facing and lining generally have a distinctive colour – it could be awkward if someone asked about the buttons and you did not know which hunt they represented. As with White Tie, decorations may be worn.

Women should dress glamorously, preferably in a long ball gown – it is after all a ball rather than a dance. It is sensible not to choose a gown that is tight or restrictive as women occasionally have to join in things like the 'Horn Blowing Competition' and need to take very deep breaths. So nothing too low or revealing in front.

Regimental Dress

For men this means exactly that: serving officers wear appropriate mess kit; others wear White Tie (although Black Tie can be worn).

For women, long is correct but short evening gowns areacceptable.

'Mess kit' is worn by members of certain senior yacht clubs. The kit is unique to each club and worn at all that club's formal functions. It should never be worn to other clubs, other than by current flag officers invited as such to another club. For example if a flag officer of, say, The Royal Thames Yacht Club is invited in his capacity as flag officer to a formal occasion at the Royal Yacht Squadron, he is entitled to wear his club's mess kit.

Cocktail Dress

For a man this means a lounge suit, unless he is continuing to a more formal event.

For women it means dress smart, be that cocktail dress, smart suit, evening trousers and silk blouse, or cashmere ensemble. The accent is on looking as if you have made an effort by dressing for an early evening that extends to dinner and who knows what. With me, that generally means being the last to leave the dance floor at Annabels, so I dress with that fact in mind.

Gloria Huniford, Robin Anderson and Liz Brewer at a Christmas dinner party in honour of Dame Shirley Bassey.
Photograph: James Peltekian

Morning Dress

This means morning or frock coat worn with plain shirt, waistcoat, stiff, white, preferably detachable collar, striped, fancy, or houndstooth trousers, and plain black shoes with laces. It is correct to wear a top hat either in grey or black depending on the colour of the coat. This is the normal attire for weddings, Royal Ascot and certain state and civic grand occasions, as indicated, when black is de rigeur. Note that grey coat is worn with matching trousers.

Women should he elegantly dressed in either a chic suit or a beautiful dress with hat and gloves.

Informal

Depending on the occasion, dress to suit the location, type of celebration and the time of day.

Smart Casual means precisely that.

Liz Brewer with Pauline Quirke, Rolf Harris and Linda Robson while filming *Jobs for the Girls – Doing a Charity Event*.

FORMS OF ADDRESS

The degree of formality with which you address someone will depend on your degree of friendship. However, as a rule, the addressee should be styled formally on an envelope regardless of how well you know him or her. The following is a brief guide to social styles of address: it is by no means comprehensive. When in doubt, consult *Whitaker's Almanack* or *Who's Who* or *Debrett's Correct Form* and stick to the formal address.

The Royal Family

Note that in sending an invitation to, or replying to an invitation from, a member of the Royal Family, you correspond with the individual's Private Secretary, not the individual directly. In making introductions, you present a person to the member of the Royal Family; you do not mention the royal person's name.

The Queen

Addressing in person: 'Your Majesty'; thereafter 'Ma'am' (pronounced Mam not Marm)

Making an introduction: 'Your Majesty, may I present...'

Addressing an envelope: The Private Secretary to Her Majesty The Queen

Starting the letter: Dear Sir (or of course Madam if the Private Secretary is a woman)

The Duke of Edinburgh

Addressing in person: 'Your Royal Highness'; thereafter 'Sir'

Making an introduction: 'Your Royal Highness, may I present...'

Addressing an envelope: The Private Secretary to His Royal Highness The Duke of Edinburgh

Starting the letter: (As for The Queen)

Royal prince and princess

Addressing in person: 'Your Royal Highness', thereafter 'Sir' or 'Ma'am'

Making an Introduction: 'Your Royal Highness, may I present...'

Addressing an envelope: The Private Secretary to His/Her Royal Highness (followed by full title, e.g., The Princess Royal, The Duke of York, Prince Michael of Kent)

Starting the letter: (As for The Queen)

Peers

Duke and duchess

Addressing in person: Duke/Duchess

Making an introduction: The Duke/Duchess of Place

Addressing an envelope: The Duke/Duchess of Place

Starting the letter : Dear Sir/Madam; or Dear Duke/Duchess of Place

Marquess and marchioness

Addressing in person: Lord/Lady Place

Making an introduction: Lord/Lady Place

Addressing an envelope: The Marquess/Marchioness of Place
Starting the letter: Dear Lord/Lady Place

Earl and countess

Addressing in person: Lord/Lady Place
Making an introduction: Lord/Lady Place
Addressing an envelope: The Earl/Countess of Place
Starting the letter: Dear Lord/Lady Place

Viscount and viscountess

Addressing in person: Lord/Lady Name
Making an introduction: Lord/Lady Name
Addressing an envelope: The Viscount/Viscountess Name
Starting the letter: Dear Lord/Lady Name

Baron and baron's wife

Addressing in person: Lord/Lady Name
Making an introduction: Lord/Lady Name
Addressing an envelope: The Lord/Lady Name
Starting the letter: Dear Lord/Lady Name

Sons and daughters of peers

Elder sons of dukes, marquesses and earls often hold courtesy titles (e.g., Earl of Place's eldest son might be styled Viscount Otherplace). Daughters and younger sons of dukes and marquesses are usually styled The Lord/Lady First & Family-Name (as is the daughter of an earl); they are addressed in person as Lord/Lady First-name.

The sons and daughters of viscounts and barons, and the younger sons of earls, usually have the style 'The Honourable', frequently shortened to 'The Hon.' before their names:

Addressing in person: Mr or Miss Family-Name, or John/Jane Family-Name
Making an introduction: It is usual to drop the Hon. unless the occasion is formal, in which case the Master of Ceremonies will announce the full name and title

Addressing an envelope: The Hon. John/Jane Family-Name
Starting a letter: Dear Mr/Miss Family-Name

Note that the wife of The Hon. John Family-Name is styled The Hon. Mrs John Family-Name (not by her own first name).

If a daughter with the style 'The Hon' marries a non-titled person (e.g., Mr John Smith), she retains her title before his surname and does not use his first name, e.g., The Hon. Mrs Smith. A son styled The Hon. remains so regardless of whether or not he is married (unless of course he inherits a main title).

Baronets and Knights

Baronet and baronet's wife
Addressing in person: Sir John (wife: Lady Smith)
Making an introduction: Sir John (wife: Lady Smith)
Addressing an envelope: Sir John Smith Bt. (wife: Lady Smith)
Starting the letter : Dear Sir John (wife: Dear Lady Smith)

Knights

Addressing in person: As for Baronet
Making an introduction: As for Baronet
Addressing an envelope: Sir John Smith (wife: Lady Smith)
Starting the letter : As for Baronet

Dames

Addressing in person: Dame Mary
Making an introduction: Dame Mary Smith
Addressing an envelope: Dame Mary Smith
Starting a letter: Dear Dame Mary

Other Titles and Styles

The scope of this book does not permit a guide to the many other titles and styles that are determined by office – members of the government and diplomatic service, the clergy, the armed services, the legal and medical professions, and so on. If you are in doubt as to how to style someone but you do not have access to an appropriate reference book, the smart thing is to call the person's office or PA and ask.

DIVORCEES

This can be a difficult area. Some women revert to their maiden names after divorce. At the time of my own divorce, my business was in my maiden name and so it made sense for me to do this. I don't particularly like the prefix Ms but accept it when necessary as I do not like to be called Mrs Liz Brewer and I am certainly not a Miss!

However, unless you know how the person prefers to be styled, the correct (and safest) way to address a divorced woman is as for a married woman, except that when formally addressing an envelope you use the woman's own first name rather than her husband's (Mrs Mary Smith, not Mrs John Smith).

A former wife of an hereditary peer is styled as though she were still married, except that her Christian name precedes her title, so the Duchess of Somewhere becomes Mary, Duchess of Somewhere, as with the late Margaret, Duchess of Argyll (note the all-important comma).

WIDOWS

Widows are addressed as for married women. It is incorrect to use the woman's own first name rather than her late husband's (unless you know she prefers it) as it can imply that the marriage ended prior to the death of her husband.

The widow of an hereditary peer or a baronet usually has 'Dowager' before the title, so the Marchioness of Somewhere becomes The Dowager Marchioness of Somewhere, Lady Name becomes Dowager Lady Name. In some cases, the widow prefers not to use the word Dowager and instead to be styled Mary, Marchioness of Somewhere.

Untitled People

Formal address for all untitled men is Mr Surname, except when addressing an envelope when the full name can be used followed by Esq (John Smith Esq). Note that Mr and Esq cannot be used at the same time.

Married women are addressed as Mrs Surname, except when addressing an envelope when the husband's full name is preceded by Mrs (Mrs John Smith).

Unmarried couples

When inviting a couple who are partners but not married, it is correct to call them by their own names unless they inform you otherwise. For example:

Sir Benjamin Slade Bt and Kirsten Hughes

or

Mr Tristan Bailey and Christiane Kahrmann

In both cases I would omit any prefix for the woman (unless she tells me to do otherwise): it seems a bit daft to include one given that she is not strictly a Miss – since she is known as part of a couple – but she is not strictly a Mrs either.

index